Idol Life

By Gretchen Huff
Pressbooks
Self-publishing

This book was produced using PressBooks.com, and PDF rendering was done by PrinceXML.

"Those who trust in themselves are fools, but
those who walk in wisdom are kept safe. . . .
For the foolishness of God is wiser than human
wisdom, and the weakness of God is stronger than
human strength."
Proverbs 28:26 and 1 Corinthians 1:25

Contents

Contents

Two idols sit on the shelf of my heart; they are named, "the expectations I have for myself" and "the expectations others have for me."

They are often at odds, and this presents me with tough choices; but, ultimately, the real conflict rears its head when these two are not in line with what God expects of me. Sometimes these idols whisper: "I must accomplish more to be worthy of love and acceptance." Sometimes they take the opposite tack: "I am content to watch this part of life pass me by, making a shallow impact on this world because no one expects much of me." Either way, these idols distract from God's promises and plans for me. I am worthy because God created me and loves me. God created me in a specific place because He has a specific purpose for my life. My own expectations are peripheral and do not deserve to sit on my heart's shelf above God's purposes. While my heart knows this truth—that my expectations should be *God's* and not *gods*—my flesh fights for my own desires.

The fight can be downright childish at times. Have you ever seen a toddler attempting to remain at Chuck E. Cheese® while his parents are valiantly trying to convince him it's time to leave? Perhaps you, too, will see the correlation, and feel the sting of familiarity: He fusses. He flails. He grips onto one of the mountainous fiberglass flashing electronic games that gobbles up currency in a flash. He is *determined* to stay put because, in his little mind, this place is the be-all end-all in fun. While his parents, being infinitely wiser in the ways of life and the world, understand that we cannot spend all of our time or money at "The Cheese," to the child there will *never* be another place he would rather spend his days. You may be chuckling at the mental picture, but we are often the adult image of that flailing three-year-old.

We may not have set our minds on pizza and flashing games, but we all have an idea of "where we want to be in life." This is not necessarily a physical place (though it might be), but a social, financial, career, or relationship state. We paint ideal images of the ultimate family, friend, romantic, and work relationship scenarios and we dream about our homes, children, and futures. But sometimes God has different plans for us. And, sometimes, we feel that our own plans are *so* much better. Our current situation or our dreamed of future paths seem like a utopia of perfection, "the Cheese" to our over-excited toddler. However, God—in His infinite wisdom—knows a better way, a way that impacts eternity, even if we cannot readily see that impact. We have a choice: to hang onto our own ideas, flailing, kicking, and protesting. Or to move forward, following God's will for us.

This battle against our selfish will, this flesh-fighting, is nothing new. For thousands of years, God's followers have warred against their own desires. Although God made David king of the Isrealites—and even testified that "I have found

David, son of Jesse a man after my own heart; he will do everything I want him to do" (Acts 13:22)—David's life was a continual battle against his own desires and expectations, that conflicted with God's. Later, Peter battled his own fear and faulty expectations when he denied Jesus three times during His arrest, trial, and ensuing crucifixion. However, despite this, Jesus reinstated Peter and confirmed his place in building the church (John 21:15-25). These two examples and countless others give me hope when I temporarily let my own expectations, in conflict with God's plans, become idols in my life. They are also a constant reminder of God's intimate knowledge of us, and of His overwhelming grace.

THIS BOOK WAS PRODUCED USING

PRESSBOOKS.COM

Easily turn your manuscript into

EPUB *Nook, Kobo, and iBooks*

Mobi *Kindle*

PDF *Print-on-demand and digital distribution*

PRESSBOOKS.COM

Simple Book Production

Chapter 1

Recall the character of Fantine in the famed musical, *Les Miserables*: while her childhood hopes of love and a forgiving god gave way to a harsh reality of injustice and survival, God's forgiveness and grace, exhibited in the character of Jean Valjean, were lavished on her daughter Cosette. Much like Fantine, we begin dreaming of our ideal lives when we are very young, before our innocent high hopes are not fulfilled in the ways we imagined. We girls name our future children when we play with dolls; we envision and discuss our future husbands, homes, and careers. "When I'm 16," we say, "I'm going to..." We lay out dreams and goals for what our lives will look like in one year, five years, and ten years. In school we are indoctrinated by the posters that hang on the walls of our classroom: "If you Believe, You Can Achieve." "The Body Achieves What the Mind Believes." "Follow Your Dreams, Fulfill Your Destiny." These posters are meant to inspire students to think about their futures and make wise decisions that will lead to opportunity for them down the road. In that way, these messages are redeeming and important. However, in another way, they can be crushing unless we have faith in God our Creator. What if we work really hard but don't achieve the job, spouse, title, or house we'd originally envisioned?

Each year we live is a new lesson in life, dreams, goals, and expectations about how things should or will turn out. When the unexpected happens, when our current reality doesn't live up to our vision of how things should be, we are tempted to anger, disillusionment, or despair. Sometimes the "unexpected" things that happen shouldn't come as a surprise—those unwelcome circumstances are the result of our own poor choices, or the poor choices of others. But what about the unexpected circumstances that we *didn't* bring on ourselves? My friend Cara * was laid off from her dream ministry job a few years ago because of a lack of funds to pay her salary. Another friend's husband left her for the mistress of country music fame. David, who had a lucrative coaching career that enabled him to successfully mentor young men, was fired because the win/loss ratio was not as high as his employer expected. My dear friend, Amber, lost her 17-month-old baby girl to an aggressive cancer. These are the kind of circumstances that most threaten to topple our faith. They are the heart-wrenching and gut-wrenching twists and turns of life, the valleys that can tear us apart. Our circumstances, though, are not a measure of our faith. When devastating events spiral out of our control, our faith in God either grows stronger or we rebel and slip away into the world's embrace.

*Some names have been changed

When we hold on too tightly to relationships, jobs, or things, we are often hesitant to let go when God comes calling, ready to lead us into something we didn't expect. This is where we make a heart decision: we can yield to God and let Him work through our unexpected circumstances, trials, or grief; or we can continue to blindly pursue that "one thing" we think we can't live without and get caught in the cycle of an "idol life." I'm not talking about wooden carvings on a shelf, as those are a rare temptation in contemporary Western culture. I'm speaking of the more insidious idols of selfish thinking, inflexibility, and the pursuit of what pleases us at the moment instead of what honors God and His greater purpose.

Letting go and giving control to God when He asks me to walk through the unexpected may be the single most difficult thing I am faced with. For those who fly by the seat of their pants, life changes may not be a big deal at first but even those with a more fluid mentality about time and goals are not immune to the same disappointments or heartbreaks we more rigid planners (or fantastical dreamers) succumb to. I am a "fixer" by nature; I often try to take control of situations by forming my own plans. This isn't necessarily a terrible trait, unless I am so adamantly pursuing the pictures in my own mind that I lose sight of God's expectations for me, or—even worse—believe that my way is good enough when His is best. If Jesus asks me to give up my current pursuits to "follow Him" like he instructed the rich man in Mark 10 to "give all he had to the poor and follow Him," am I willing to do that? The rich man "went away sad," the Gospel says, "because he had many possessions." Do we go away sad because we hold tight-fistedly to what we think should happen? Instead of living life with an open palm, handing over not only burdens but plans and expectations to God to see how He will bless us, we close our fists and clinch tightly to what we *want* to happen or what other people want for us. Maybe like the rich man, we miss out on a multitude of blessings, "100 times over" what we settle for.

THE FRAME OF THE WORD

When Edward Mote wrote the lyrics to the hymn "The Solid Rock" in the 1800s, he certainly wasn't anticipating that a woman in 21st century America would one day analyze its verses. He probably also wouldn't have anticipated that the popular verse—"On Christ the solid rock I stand, all other ground is sinking sand"* —would be incorporated into modern worship songs and sung across the world. He was simply an English pastor who wrote hymns to praise God and was inspired by a friend's illness to flesh out the beginnings of his poem of praise and encouragement.

When I was a girl, our Baptist congregation sang this song to piano and organ accompaniment. The cadence of it still resounds in my head as I read the lyrics silently to myself. Like most chil-

*Edward Mote. "Solid Rock." Hymns of Praise. 1836.

dren, I never thought much about the words of the hymn as I belted them out in church. I do remember loving the way the song rose in crescendo during the chorus and then gently lulled in decrescendo on "all other ground is sinking sand, all other ground is sinking sand." That last "sinking sand" was always pronounced with such finality and sadness! I knew it was bad news to build my house on it, and that I should aim for solid rock. After all, in children's church we sang, "The wise man built his house upon the rock;" and everyone knew what happened when "the foolish man built his house upon the sand"—the rains came down, the floods came up, and his house came tumbling down.

It wasn't until recently that I felt compelled to parallel these lyrics to life. In his beloved hymn, Mote encourages us to "dare not trust the sweetest frame, but wholly lean on Jesus' name." The phrase "sweetest frame" became stuck in my mind. My first thought was to associate the phrase with the physical frame of a house—the frame built on Jesus as your foundation is solid, while a house built on anything else is open to sinking, blowing over, or simply collapsing when the storms come. But a "frame" also surrounds a photo or piece of art and holds it for display. Sometimes we "frame" the picture of our lives with cultural ideas, theories, or guidelines that don't follow the teachings of Jesus. If our ideas aren't centered in Christ, we find ourselves constantly trying to "straighten out" our picture frames as they slide askew on the walls of our lives. When we find ourselves asking, "What is the purpose? Why am I here? Does any of this even matter?" it's time to step back and evaluate. We may be living an "idol life," consumed with things or circumstances that overshadow Christ's call.

As people in a postmodern era, we are all about plans, ideas, and theories. We are bombarded by a culture that pushes certain expectations on us. We are prone to bend and bow to the expectations and opinions of the people around us if we aren't surrounding ourselves with God's Word, wise mentors, and friends who are encouraging us to pursue the Lord wholeheartedly. Some of these cultural expectations are easily spotted—"Do whatever it takes to become materially wealthy," or "Look out for number one." It may seem logical that we should pursue wealth, watch our backs, and do what we can for ourselves; but God tells us to "love the Lord your God with all of your heart, soul, and mind" (Matthew 22:37) and "love others and serve them"(Matthew 22:38). His Word teaches us to live with integrity and not to speak falsely about others.

Other prevalent cultural adages are sneakier in that they sound so positive: "Do what makes you happy," or "All I've ever wanted is for you to be happy." The pursuit of happiness permeates our culture and threatens to take over our love and devotion to God. Like all emotions, happiness continually ebbs and flows. If our lives are focused only on the pursuit of it, we will be tossed by every wave, led astray by every breeze that harbors the promise of heightened spirits.. Happiness alone cannot be a solid foundation upon which to build a frame for life.

I am still learning that the key to contentment and peace, in the presence or absence of happiness, is living to fulfill *God's* expectations for me, not my own or other people's. I am learning that His expectations are lighter to carry than those the world puts on me, but are initially more challenging to my faith. Jesus said, "...my yoke is easy and my burden is light" (Matthew 11:30). It's easy and light because He carries it with us! Many people in your life may have high expectations for you, but they aren't often willing to help you meet them. We are often just as hard on ourselves. We lay out goals for ourselves with very short amounts of time to meet them, then become disheartened when we miss our self-imposed deadline. Jesus asks us to take up our cross and follow Him, but He has carried the burden of it Himself. His cross was literal, ours is only symbolic. He endured the actual pain of the cross; we have only to follow what it stands for—grace, sacrifice, and love. What may seem "unreliable" to the world around us—faith in a loving God we cannot see and belief in his Son, Jesus Christ—is actually the most solid foundation to build upon (Hebrews 11:1-3).

As I framed my children's school pictures recently, I paid attention to the contrast of the light cherry wood of the frame, it's black accents, and how both details served to highlight and contrast with the photographs' colors. What if we a frame our daily lives and decisions with God's Word, in order to test the foundation? Does the frame surrounding and supporting the fabric of our lives center in Christ or in worldly culture? Maybe we've never considered how much culture and nature can influence the way we think and the decisions we make. We may have trouble sifting through the sand of what everybody else expects of us, to find the rock of God's expectations. The ultimate sifter for any believer is God's Word. He has given us everything we need to live in a relationship with Him. His word is full of principles, commands, and guidelines, all bound by His mercy and His unfailing love—and the totality of His nature is key. If we think God is only the God of boundaries, then we tend to either rebel against those boundaries (and God Himself), or strive to become "good enough" to please God. Neither picture is what God has framed for us. If we think God is only the God of love—as we think of "love" in Western culture—we are misled. He gives us unfailing grace and love but also guides us in ways that protect us from hurt and regret, rather than hinder our talents and gifts.

BIBLICAL EXAMPLES

It's easy to get distracted by things that look good. In our American culture that stresses comfort and luxury, our "life pictures" often resemble a glossy magazine layout. We are also distracted by the fictional "idyllic relationships" we read about in books and watch on the big screen. Romantic pictures of perfection are fictional. Relationships involve people and *all* people are broken. When we find ourselves going against God's Word in order to attain these pictures, we are ultimately in sinking sand; no matter how idyllic our life appears from the outside in. We may not sink immediately, and may look wildly successful to the world, but the solid foundation isn't there. And here's the kicker—God often calls us to do things and begin friendships that look downright insane to others.

God's Word gives us examples of strong ancestors in the faith whose life-pictures were radically changed as they followed God, and who at times looked unsuccessful, if not downright crazy. These are the patriarchs and matriarchs of our current faith. We are sometimes tempted to look at them as no more than historic or symbolic figures, but they were real people—real followers of God—who had to live in harmony with their siblings, parents, spouses, children, and neighbors. They had daily tasks to perform, just like we do, and they had expectations placed on their lives by those around them, by themselves, and by God. They had to answer the questions of others because of their unusual choices. But because these men and women followed God, their foundations weren't shaken, even in the midst of literal and figurative storms.

Noah, who had already lived for 600 years (Genesis 7:6), was asked to perform a task that seemed insurmountable: he had to build a boat the size of three football fields to house eight adults and countless land animals for over a month. (The sheer size of the ark and the looming task of gathering wild animals would have been enough to put me off and ignite my complaining nature!) Not only did he have to complete this giant task, he was performing it in the total faith that God was going to do something He'd never done before. Noah did not let his surrounding culture of corruption (Genesis 6:5, 11) influence him. Noah continued building his house of faith on solid rock. He walked with God. As a result, he and his family alone survived the flood to repopulate earth.

Abraham, who had a pretty good life in his hometown, trusted God enough to take a journey to an unknown land and begin a new life. Abraham had "no inheritance [there], not even enough ground to set his foot on" and was childless, but God had promised him that he and his descendants would possess the land (Acts 7:5). If you've ever trusted a promise of God without immediate, tangible results to that obedience, you're not alone. Abraham, the father of the Jewish and Christian nations, led the way.

Ruth, a young widow, journeyed with her mother-in-law to a foreign place (Ruth 1:16) and put her life in the hands of a stranger whose customs and beliefs were unknown to her. Her obedience to the God of the Hebrews and her lack of fear led her to a husband who cared for her and incorporated her into the very family tree of Jesus

Christ (Ruth 4:17). Ruth could have easily stayed in her culture and lived according to its expectations, but she would have missed God's blessing for her life—a blessing she never could have imagined while mourning in Moab.

Sarah and Elizabeth from the Old and New Testament stories were both barren. They had expectations at one time that they would have children but, as the years passed, their disappointments influenced them. God ultimately brought about His plan in the lives of both women—they both bore sons who were integral parts of God's plan. But Sarah doubted God and at first took matters into her own hands (Genesis 16:1-4). She put her life picture in a frame of her own making. Although she eventually had the child God promised her, her attempt to control God's plan for her had serious consequences (see Hagar, Ishmael, and his descendants). On the other hand, Elizabeth was consistently faithful to God. Her life was framed by His Promises and her faith. As a result, she was blessed with a promised son (Luke 1:13-17) and was a blessing to those around her—even the mother of Jesus.

None of these famous followers of God were perfect. Let's not misinterpret what it means to build your foundation on the rock of God or to frame your life picture with His Word. All of the matriarchs and patriarchs of faith were flawed. They made mistakes. They faced trials and suffered the consequences of their disobedience or unbelief. It is safe to speculate that none of their lives followed the path *they* had originally envisioned for themselves; however, God used each one and blessed them because, fundamentally, their faith was in Him—He was the rock and the framer of these famous lives. They believed God and it was credited unto them as righteousness (Genesis 15:6). In our modern culture, we often succumb to the messages of media, the opinions of those around us, and the pervading call to "do what makes you happy" when framing our lives. When our life picture is framed in Christ, we may seem "old-fashioned" or "crazy" to those around us, but it is our calling to be set apart. Our security is in our Creator, and His Word promises that He is working for our good even if we can't *immediately* see it.

ONE WOMAN'S MIND

Now that I have referenced God's Word, let me be transparent. I am a woman with expectations and goals. I want to encourage my children and husband, but there are days when I am negative and caustic. I have a goal of writing and publishing a book, but busy-work, home projects, or television often distract me. I have an expectation that I should be teaching in some capacity, because I believe God gifted me with the ability, but I have at times been so focused on it that I have taken control of what that looks like, instead of letting God show me. I cannot deny my German/Midwestern roots, nor the personality and expectations that are part of my DNA, but I can't blame all of my tendencies towards busyness, planning, and control on my inherited traits. I still have a choice.

Planners and task-oriented people get things done. We have our place in society and tend to believe, from the bottom of our hearts, that society would fall apart without us. We have to purposefully take time to be still and know that God is God and we are not. I have to actually *think* about reaching out to people, whereas I have friends who can talk to people easily. We type-A folks who are also introverts have to *make* ourselves sit down and have long conversations; it's not our natural "go-to" mode. I have been envious, more than once, of my friends who come by conversation naturally. They speak to everyone they meet. These extroverts always seem to know the right thing to say, and are usually more concerned with the well-being of people than with the cleanliness level of their bathrooms or whether they will have time to vacuum out the car. And here is an area where I struggle. God has called me to relationship with Him and others. People are created in His image and are of the utmost importance to Him. I really do want to have God's love for people, to ask people how they are doing and focus on the answer, but I am often ineffective. I am an expert at accomplishing a to-do list and can multi-task with the best of them, but only power and grace—and God's expectation for me to love people—keep me from being a lonely girl who finishes a lot of tasks, without any real purpose. People *are* the purpose.

Why would tasks matter at all, without other humans?

I could easily get caught up in my natural inclination to make lists, check off what's been done, and move on to the next item, while putting the people and eternal work God has placed in my life on the back burner. For the record, list-making is not without merit (see my tendency to defend my task-oriented self!), but for someone like me, even mental checklists can consume me to the point of neglecting my relationships. When I look at Jesus's life, I can't help seeing that He invested in *people*. He was focused on those around Him, what they needed, and how He could help them grow. He personally invested in twelve men and several women and spent most of His time with people—teaching them, praying for them, and, most of all, loving them. Many of us know the story of Mary and Martha, Lazarus's sisters. They were among Jesus's closest friends. Jesus gently chastised Martha at one point for being so wrapped up in her tasks that she didn't take time for relationship (Luke 10:38-41). I *am* a Martha. I've even done a Bible study by Joanna Weaver entitled *Being a Mary in a Martha World*. It was a great study but, alas, it didn't magically change my personality; to change my behaviors and make people more central than tasks in my life takes effort. But this is God's expectation for me. His greatest command is to love Him and love people, and that often requires putting a task aside and just listening. At the end of the day, that might mean some of the items on my to-do list remain unchecked. That's okay. God is re-framing my expectations.

To counteract my own tendency to take control of my life—to follow my own flesh-controlled goals, and to put tasks first and people last—I have framed my life with God's Word. I pray for Him to show me people who need love and that He will help me give that love to them. I pray each day for the trust to make decisions that might seem crazy to my culture, but are pleasing to God. During this season, I feel God has screeched my type-A life to a halt and is leading me down a path that has forced me to look at my relationships with people and discern what is most important. I am learning to praise God in the midst of circumstances in which I must be still. He is teaching me that He is the rock upon which I can build my foundation, and that His expectations for me are to live humbly, love others, and walk with Him. If I rely on my checklists alone—or on all of the goals my culture expects me to have—I may as well stand on quicksand in the middle of a downpour. Yet I know that if I stand on the rock of God, He will quiet me in the midst of the storms of my busy life, and will remind me of what is most important.

CALLED TO THE UNKNOWN

I am sitting, at 3:30 am, frantically typing before an idea rolls away like the tide. I am doing this, partly, because I was the idiot who forgot to turn my ringer to vibrate while my cell phone charged beside my bed. Those crazy emailed daily advertisements are partly to blame for me being wide awake (thanks Constant Contact®!); but let's be real—the other thing responsible for this wakefulness is a small anxiety that burns like a candle flame in my gut.

This tiny flicker was lit when I resigned from my full-time teaching job in order to write a book and focus more fully on my children. I truly feel this is God's expectation for me at this particular point in my life, but I'd be lying if I plastered a smile on my face and proclaimed—in my best Sunday School voice—that I have fearless and unwavering faith in this decision. It is more accurate to say that I have faith in God, despite my fears. It's hard enough when God calls us to things that don't make sense to others but, sometimes, He calls us to things that don't even make sense to *us*.

My tendency to become consumed by goals instead of taking time for family and relationships had begun to creep into my job as a high school teacher and my home life as a wife and mother—I felt that I went non-stop from sunrise to sunset simply trying to accomplish a long list of tasks. I had lost my joy in teaching. I had felt for some time that there were words inside me that God wanted me to put on paper, but, in the chaos of my daily schedule, I could never find the time to begin.

The decision to put my teaching career on hold was not an easy one. I walked my letter of resignation to the principal's office and back to the security of my classroom many times before I finally took the plunge. And although I truly do love teaching and feel it is a calling in my life, the indecision and wavering was more about money and security than current job satisfaction. I have fear issues when it comes to money, and I had become very comfortable in our financial circumstances. It was nice to have plenty to pay the bills and still have a little extra for fun stuff. Although the Bible tells us not to worry about money, we can't always prevent it. I know I am blessed to have a husband with a good job. I know that income is relative. I just can't help having panicky thoughts about financially-related matters from time to time. We all have our own fiscal expectations—how padded our savings account should be; what we should invest in; whether to work part-time, full-time, or not at all. The core of Matthew 6:30, however, promises that if we seek God first in our daily lives and habits, He will provide our needs; and not only will those financial needs be provided, but also those needs we have for companionship, relationship, and yes, even time to complete our list.

DIVINE PEACE

God expects us, whether we work outside of our homes or within, to put our faith in Him, even when the candle flame of worry starts burning in the pits of our stomachs. If we are following God, and living lives of integrity, He will put callings on our lives and create different routes to accomplish them. God will never lead us contrary to His Word, but these callings will not look the same for different people, nor will they be worked out the same way in our lives.

It is far too easy to make thin slips of green-printed currency our true love, and slip into an idol life. As American believers, we are surrounded by a culture that constantly compares. Some of us are more inclined to do this than others, depending on our upbringing or social circle, but if we're honest, we all fall prey to the temptation at least occasionally. We look at our financial situation, or even our faith and say, "Well, I'm *ahead* of this person, but *behind* that one." All this accomplishes is to make us worried that we aren't "keeping up" or to make us forgetful of those with needs if we are "way ahead." We often measure our path by the path of others—but God just doesn't work that way. Because He has created us all uniquely, and has given us different gifts and talents, we are all positioned in different places intentionally. We experience different circumstances (and that includes financial ones) to accomplish His greater purpose—to be salt and light.

When we start comparing ourselves to others instead of listening for God's voice, we often miss a step. Financially, we may try to keep up with our peers by spending money we don't have. When we do, we are "bowing" to money by letting it control us, whether we realize it or not. First Timothy 6:10 warns that, "The love of money is a root of all kinds of evil." Jesus reminds us in Matthew 6:24 that we must have one master and not let our heart be divided between serving money and God.

While we are warned to guard our hearts against the love of money, it's not the only trap we face in attempting to "keep up." Some of us "play perfect" pretending everything is roses all of the time. We lack authenticity and transparency because we want others to think we have perfect lives. Spiritually, we look at someone's walk and expect a similar experience for ourselves. We judge our relationship with God in comparison or contrast to theirs. Comparisons to others or facades of perfection only lead me to pride, disillusionment, or discontent. I read a quote in Oswald Chamber's *My Utmost for His Highest* that speaks to this tendency:

"One of the hardest lessons to learn comes from our stubborn refusal to refrain from interfering in other people's lives. It takes a long time to realize the danger of being an amateur Providence, that is, interfering with God's plan for others." *

We are tempted to judge others (those we deem superior and inferior to ourselves) because they are living out God's will for them differently than we are; or we judge ourselves because God is fulfilling His purpose in us in a different manner than He is in our friends. God did not make me like everyone else. He did not make you like everyone else, either. He has planted specific desires, callings, and talents in each of us that He wants us to use. Sometimes when we use them, we will

---

*Oswald Chambers. My Utmost for His Highest. (Discovery House Publishers, 1992)

be "successful" in the eyes of others. Other times, the world will wonder what we are thinking. If our foundation is solidly built on God, it doesn't matter one way or the other.

There are believers who fully embrace their calling and never look back. They never seem to second-guess what God has called them to. I wish I were always one of those people, but I am not. I go through cycles. I experience seasons of great confidence and seasons of doubt; seasons of contentment and seasons of discontent. That is why God said clearly through Solomon that we are to "Trust in the Lord with all [our] hearts and lean not on [our] own understanding; in all [our] ways submit to Him, and He will make [our] paths straight" (Proverbs 3:5). God knows us intimately (Psalm 139:13-16). He knows in our flesh that we will struggle to trust in a God we can't see. As Paul said, "Not that I have already accomplished these things but ... I press on toward the goal to win the prize for which God has called me heavenward in Christ Jesus" (Philippians 3:12, 15). I am still learning to listen to God's voice *first,* learning to press on toward the goal. Right now, part of that "pressing" is writing. Sharing a deep part of ourselves with others can be the ultimate test in letting go and letting God. So here I am—writing away, even though I still have bouts of fear along my current path. I've learned I can trust and follow Him, even when fear strikes; I just have to keep moving ahead and He will provide. I stand on his Word — my rock, and though storms will come, my foundation will remain secure.

"WHO ARE YOU?"

The Gospel of Mark is a rediscovered treasure. The shortest of the narratives of Jesus's life and teachings has some amazing details. In Chapter 3, we learn that Jesus had many followers and only called those that He "wanted" to be his twelve disciples. Mark tells us that, while Jesus only spoke in parables or symbolic stories to the masses, He explained everything to the disciples. But although the disciples witnessed miracle upon miracle, and were flat-out *told* by Jesus that He was the Messiah, they still didn't "get it." They didn't get it because their expectations were not being met. It wasn't that Jesus didn't merit their praise—He healed terminally ill people and calmed the stormy waters after walking on them; He spoke with wisdom, knowledge, and authority; He exhibited extreme patience and exceeded anything they could have imagined with humility and a servant's attitude. The problem was that the disciples, along with the rest of the Jewish nation, were looking for an earthly king.

When Jesus rode into Jerusalem on a colt, he was greeted like a king. The citizens laid palm branches on the road and waved them, yelling, "Hosanna! Blessed is he who comes in the name of the Lord!" (Mark 11:9). As the week unfolded, and the events leading to the cross played out as God had always intended, the people lost their admiration and faith and turned against Jesus. It was impossible for them to see how big God's plan was. They wanted someone who fit into their narrow religious traditions and historical teachings, and would also physically conquer the Roman Empire. Jesus *did* fit the prophecies, and perfectly, but they couldn't see it because His battle was fought in the spiritual realm rather than the physical one. They were not expecting humility. They were not expecting service. They were not expecting their "king" to bow his head and accept a humiliating death. The Jewish people had been waiting for a traditional leader to conquer their oppressors. Jesus, however, was fulfilling a much higher calling.

The disciples couldn't see what was right in front of them because they had no vision for what Jesus would ultimately accomplish. We can't really blame them. How often have we plodded along, following a path that we have chosen or that has been chosen for us, expecting something on our "known" plane of greatness—only to miss an extraordinary blessing of God happening right in front of our faces? Like the disciples, we are so sure of what to expect from Christ—something that looks and feels familiar, that fits with our culture and doesn't rock the boat too much—that we often miss glimpses of glory that Christ holds right in front of us. We too often prefer to continue on the route of our own making; in control, relying totally on self, calling all of the shots, making idols of our own plans, living for our own expectations instead of seeking God's.

God doesn't give up on us—whether our idols are tangible objects or intangible ideologies, whether our gods are named or theoretical—God never stops pursuing us, loving us, and calling us to seek Him, trust Him, live his expectations for us and become whole, standing on rock.

Chapter 2

Expectations of Life

MOTHERHOOD

Nine years ago, standing with toes on the firm sand of the water's edge on a blindingly white beach, the ocean breeze caressing my skin, I looked out across the Gulf of Mexico and inhaled the deep scent of salty air. For a moment, I was serene, relaxed, and happy. In the blink of an eye, the tide hollowed out the sand around my feet and the waves sent me crashing face-first into the surf. No major physical damage was done, outside of a couple of bloody knees and scraped palms, but I was shaken. This "perfect" environment had literally toppled me!

I remember this incident so vividly because, at the time, I was expecting my first child. I have always been convinced that God is literary and appreciates symbolism and foreshadowing as much as I do. This crash into the surf was the work of a skillful author indeed—the birth of my first child really rocked my world. I was 31 and had been married for two years; I felt pretty "in control" of my life. When Ben came on the scene, I was suddenly responsible for this tiny human life—it was overwhelming. The first few months of his life were a grand lesson in building my foundation on the rock and not on myself, worldly wisdom, or any other theory. That tumble into the sandy beach of Gulf Shore, Florida, was just a precursor to let me know that while life with kids is messy (and can knock you off your feet at times) it is still beautiful. I struggled for a time over what seemed a lull in my relationship with God. I let myself become overwhelmed by lack of sleep, around the clock feedings, and the general neediness of my newborn son. The time I used to have for myself had vanished and Ben had taken over. Because I felt I was not longer in control, it translated in my head that God was no longer in control: enter a hands-on, palpable lesson from God. When I let go of my control is when God shows Himself the most. In hindsight I realized I was always in His hand. I needed a season of more focused energy on the baby He'd placed in my care to teach me how to lose myself for awhile. Instead of relying on myself or taking my cues from the world, I trusted God's grace and quit worrying about living the picture-perfect mom life.

When the sands of our lives shift, and a once-innocuous tide catches us off guard and dumps us unceremoniously into the sand, serenity and relaxation can turn instantly into so much sand scratching around in our swimsuits. If my foundation is the Rock of Ages, then the sand in my swimsuit is merely a wake-up call; a gentle loving nudge, not a call to change the frame of my theology or the purpose of my life. During my children's infancy and toddlerhood I had to learn what it meant to have a small person totally rely on me and my capacity to provide and make wise decisions. We are *so* closely attached to our children that we take all of their moods, actions, and decisions personally. We feel responsible for all of the little bad things that pop up but often forget to revel in the joys. As a task-oriented mom, I had to continually remind myself that my children would only be babies for a brief season. I needed to soak it up.

Whether we've thought about it or not, we've all stretched our parenting picture over a frame. A couple may have prepared a big ornate mental frame ready to hold a professional portrait of their large family and yet have no children. Perhaps they struggle to understand why God has not granted them the children they expected, feeling purposeless in that area of their lives. Or maybe their dream was to have a houseful of kids and they have only one. Our desired family pictures may shift, but if our frame remains steady in the Lord, He can paint a work of art in His own design. God's work in our lives is like a jigsaw puzzle. Each piece is integral, but without the other pieces, the picture will never be complete. If just one piece is missing, an observer will still be able to make out the picture, but the totality of the image will be incomplete. God sees the entire puzzle of our lives, completely, before we're born. We live our lives piece by piece. We tend to get hung up on one piece sometimes and base all of our decisions on that one piece. That piece can even be our child. We are called by God to care for and nurture our children. He places them in our lives with the responsibility of teaching them, and helping them grow, but when we idolize our children, or bow to our expectations concerning them instead of trusting God's plan for them and for us, we end up face-first in the sand.

THE WOMAN IN THE "MOM HAT"

In a parenting expectation parallel, I was wondering the other day how the man with the yellow hat feels—you know, the guy who spends his life with Curious George. On the popular PBS show that my children loved, the man with the yellow hat has no name; he's defined only by his fashion sense and the fact that he owns a very curious monkey. Everyone around him constantly talks to George and about George, but no one ever addresses George's owner by name. In the books and on the show, he is merely the nameless caretaker of a prodigious mammal. While musing over this one summery Friday morning as my daughter wrapped up her 30-minute session in front of the television, I realized that moms can feel just like the nameless man in the yellow hat.

As mothers, we move through the gambit of emotional joy when we find out we are expecting or that the adoption papers have gone through. We carry our children safely inside us for nine months or patiently in our hearts while we pray and correspond with various adoption officials; we wait for the day motherhood becomes real, by physical or emotional labor. While we wait, we plan, dream, decorate nurseries and kid rooms, and begin stocking our homes and closets with tiny apparel. After all, we don't say we're "expecting" for nothing. We have visions of how our children will look, act, interact, and grow. We have hopes, dreams, plans, and expectations for them *and* ourselves. Those expectations rarely include the less desirable realities of motherhood: bone-tiredness from multiple late-night feedings; the seemingly impossible multiplication of loads of laundry; the degeneration of our wardrobes from stylish dressing to sweats, old t-shirts, maternity jeans way past our due dates; and the pervading new perfume that fills the house—one part spit up, two parts dirty diaper. These are the minor startling realities of birthing a completely healthy child. Sometimes those realities of motherhood are much more serious: your long-awaited baby may have a heart defect, Down Syndrome, cerebral palsy, or autism; he or she may develop cancer or another life-threatening illness. No little girl dreams of these sorts of harsh realities while dressing her dolly or pushing her toy stroller.

As these motherhood realities—minor and serious—sink in, it's easy to let them affect our relationships and lose our sense of who we are in Christ. Major complications in the lives of our children are a grand weapon used to knock our faith out. Many women become so consumed with their babies and young children (a natural tendency) that they refuse to leave them in anyone else's care. They're so concerned with nourishing their children, they forget to nourish themselves — physically and spiritually. Others become so absorbed with getting to know the new addition to the family that they lose touch with everyone else, unable to make time to maintain their marriages or friendships. Many of us resign from our jobs to become stay-at-home moms, thus losing the identity we had through our careers. Because of our fatigue, good habits—like quiet time spent with God, regular exercise, and evenings out with the spouse—are often all but abandoned. In the midst of all of this, our identities take both a physical and spiritual hit. I remember talking to my pastor's wife when my son was a baby, telling her how disconnected I felt from God without the daily quality time spent studying His word and the loss of my teaching ministry. She reassured me by telling me the chaotic schedule was just a season of life—I still had identity in Christ. She reminded me that I still had a strong ministry; it was just to a different group of people. Despite the never-ceasing loads of laundry and constant demands of motherhood, I *was* more than just a woman in a "mom hat."

During the journey of motherhood, I have been blessed to be surrounded by women of faith. I have friends in my life who have lived every serious reality of motherhood mentioned previously. All of them have been pillars of faith, allowing God to carry them through unexpected, and sometimes devastating, circumstances. That doesn't mean they haven't grieved, mourned, struggled, or asked "Why?". It doesn't even mean they haven't cried out to God in anger, devastation, or bouts of depression or despair. What it means is that, despite their emotions and circumstances, and heartaches, they never lost sight that God was their Creator and he was in control, even if they didn't understand or still don't understand His answer to their prayers.

Our expectations for ourselves and our children are topped off by the expectations of other moms and the "one-upmanship" that seems to creep in whenever moms start comparing their children. Don't get caught up in these expectations! No matter how often we women try to put up a perfect facade, trusting God to grow you in Him does not mean you will reach perfection on earth. Neither you nor your child will *ever* be perfect. Your child will not always do as you'd hoped. You will both make mistakes. You will never have time to accomplish every task, or fulfill your children's every wish. You will not always have patience with your children, (or husband!). Sometimes you will work outside the home and provide financially, and sometimes you won't. There will be days when you feel you are juggling it all nicely and days when not one, but *all* the balls come crashing down. Not all of your decisions will be the right ones, and choices that are right for this year may not be in God's plan for the next. You and your husband may have a few wonderful years of marriage and parenting and a few difficult ones. There will be times when the "in love" feeling you had for your spouse, or your newborn baby fades, but both are replaced by a greater kind of love — an unconditional, worked for love that God grows in us, and Godly love of your children and spouse trumps trying to meet the world's expectations for parenting.

Godly love is not permissive, but it is forgiving. Godly love is not demanding, but it does have standards. Godly love never tells you to "do whatever makes you happy" but encourages you to "pursue your passions with Godly purpose." When your children see you serving God, helping people, loving your spouse, and being an encourager, it doesn't matter whether you work inside or outside the home. It doesn't matter whether you're built like Angelina Jolie or Melissa McCarthy, your children will rise and call you blessed. There will be daily struggles, but in the long run, you will have the most satisfaction and contentment if you set your expectations for yourself in God's frame and let the fact that you are His determine your identity.

Between the loss of identity, unmet expectations, and the pressure to be career women, loving mothers, and supportive wives all at the same time, heaping platters of mom guilt are served up daily. We must fight the urge to inhale them because they can leave us disillusioned and depressed. The fallout from our frustration can shower down on everyone in our paths—our children, spouses, co-workers, neighbors, friends, and strangers. But when we find our identities in Christ, those idols of unmet expectations will not consume us. As for the man in the yellow hat, he *does* exhibit patience, friendship, curiosity, and a caring nature. While we may never know his name, we know his character.

EXPECTATIONS AND IDENTITY

I've been known to let God's Word overwhelm me. I don't know about you, but I remember reading Proverbs 31:10-31 and thinking: "I need to rise before daylight every day, feed my children the most nutritious food, fill them with hope and comfort, remember to treat my husband with respect, make it to my job on time, work diligently to provide income, return home to spend quality time with and care for my family, all while making sure that they're well dressed and calling me blessed." I've *been* in the middle of working full time, raising two children, being a wife, serving in church, trying to keep the house in order, and putting healthy food on the table. I can assure you that my family was probably not calling me blessed on a daily basis. I think our error in reading Proverbs 31 comes when we focus only on the *actions* of the wife as a standard to strive for, instead of looking at her attitude and character. Here is the attitude I see in this wife of wisdom: she loves and cares for her family. She weighs the worth and usefulness of things before she purchases them. She is a woman of integrity. She doesn't embarrass her husband with her words and actions, but makes him proud of who she is.

Parenting is only one area of identity where our choice of foundation can balance our lives or fell us. Even those women who may never have children still have expectations for being a wife and a career woman. Because of this, I believe Proverbs 31 can inspire women in many different seasons of life; it is a picture for *all* women, regardless of current circumstances or culture. Do you have a career and no children? Then make wise decisions in that career and guard your heart and character. Don't let yourself be defined only as a "career woman" because that's where you currently are spending most of your time. Are you a wife? Love and assist your husband. Let his friends know you as someone who lifts him up, not tears him down; don't believe for a minute that encouraging your husband means you are a "weak woman." Do you have children? Remember your responsibility to raise them in the Lord. Love them, care for them, train them, and encourage them, but don't let your sole identity be the nameless woman in the "mommy hat." Are you single? Then despite the loneliness you sometimes feel, you have the greatest freedom of all to minister for God. Pour out the love He has for you on other people. He's given you the outlets, just recognize them. Don't for a minute believe the lie that God has overlooked you because you are not married. Don't believe that He doesn't have plans for you.

Above all, remember that we are not perfect regardless of the many hats we wear—even if we wear them well! Idolizing a picture of perfection in our own lives or family life will only lead us to despair; it is a fairy-tale state, impossible to achieve on earth. It will also alienate us from others who know the truth—that marriage, parenting, and careers are hard work! As believers, we are being changed every single day by the power of Christ, but if we are transparent, we will admit the process of change is not always pretty! The greatest wisdom is to trust Him first, to lean not on our own understanding, nor that of the world around us. He will give us the strength to keep our minds, bodies, and responsibilities in perspective. Following God and relying on His expectations for us will not bulletproof us against heartache, or safeguard us from mistakes. Relying on God will never be a "pill of perfection", but it is an oasis of peace in the midst of the worldly battle that rages around us.

When you feel that you have become defined by your striving for a perfect life, fear not! According to Proverbs 31 it is not *what* you accomplish that makes a name for you, but the *character* you display as you live. The most important words in the chapter are not the verbs, but the adjectives: "noble, good, eager, vigorous, strong, dignified, wise, faithful, blessed. If our expectations are worldly, and we label ourselves by what we're doing, we are standing on shifting sand. However, if we strive to be wise, faithful, and consistent in our spiritual lives we *will* be the wife of noble character, the career woman standing on the rock, the mom who is blessed—even through seasons of difficulty. If our focus is on loving God and loving people, we will never lose our identity as children of God, no matter what our season in life or current occupation.

APPEARANCE

Whether you're a grown woman or a teenage girl, expectations for our outward appearances can be overpowering. As a teen, or young 20 something there's so much to contend with—a boy who does not text you back, a girl who ridicules you, or a failing grade—that the added worries of a body that is not a size two or blemishes on your face is enough to send you crashing into the sand. As women, we don't stop comparing ourselves to others; not only in regards to our relationships, careers, and our children, but our looks and waistlines as well. It's easy to desire what other girls or women have, but when we get into this "comparison mode" we begin to walk down the road of bowing to beauty and tend to tighten our fists and try to take control to achieve physical perfection. All too easily in American culture, our physical appearance—or our quest to radically change it—becomes our idol.

It's not easy to open our hand and give these expectations to God. It's difficult, as a teenager, to not care what others say about your lack of a bikini body or your acne. As a grown woman and mother, it's sometimes impossible to ignore what you know or think others are saying about your muffin top or crow's feet. If you are following God's expectations for you this pressure doesn't ultimately matter—but, in the culture crunch of society, it sure feels like it does! As women, the desire to meet the world's expectations—and sense of failure if we don't—plagues us on a slightly larger scale because we're adults. We're supposed to be completely in control of our lives and appearances, right? This is where our culture can really reach out and grab us by the beauty jugular.

Body image and physical appearance have become the constant focus of television, movies, magazines, and billboards. The number of diets and patented products and procedures that cater to those who want to look thinner, prettier, or younger make up a mind-boggling multi-billion dollar industry. The world expects women to look beautiful on the outside—and there's definitely a "look" that is most preferred. From our weight and curves to our hair and makeup, the importance of physical beauty is emphasized incessantly to American women. Because of this arbitrary cultural standard, we sometimes feel like we're *failing* if we don't look like the latest magazine cover model. Because of this, we battle many issues that are related to our self-esteem, most of them caused by the way we *think* we're supposed to look.

BIBLICAL BEAUTY

Our looks, and the means by which we improve them, are sometimes a touchy subject in the Christian community. You can alight on almost any end of the spectrum. There are entire sects and denominations dedicated to teaching that women should not seek any outward means of improving their appearance—they forbid haircuts, make-up, and even colorful clothing. At the other end of the spectrum are believing women who have a huge impact for Christ while being externally beautiful and, in some cases, even making a fortune in the beauty industry. Most of us fall somewhere in between these two.

It is easy to cross lines in this area and even raise some hackles, but let's pause and consult some important Scripture before we completely box anyone in or out. One verse that fires the flames of minimalist views of beauty is 1 Peter 3:3-4:

> *Your beauty should not come from outward adornment, such as elaborate hairstyles and the wearing of gold jewelry or fine clothes. Rather, it should be that of your inner self, the unfading beauty of a gentle and quiet spirit, which is of great worth in God's sight.*

Those who advocate that women should not wear make-up or jewelry or cut their hair generally espouse these verses. On the other side of the camp, the counterargument often cites the book of Esther, which describes all of the beauty treatments she underwent before going before the king (Esther 2:12). Those familiar with the story know that Esther's physical beauty was what first gave her the opportunity to counsel with the king, which led to the salvation of the Israelite nation from the hands of Haman.

Other verses about outward appearance exist: "The Lord does not look at the things people look at. People look at the outward appearance, but the Lord looks at the heart" (1 Samuel 16:7b). "Charm is deceptive and beauty is fleeting; but a woman who fears the Lord is to be praised" (Proverbs 31:30). In Deuteronomy 21:10-11 God tells the Israelite men that they are free to marry beautiful women who capture their eye, as long as they follow God's guidelines first. And in Proverbs 11:22 we read, "Like a gold ring in a pig's snout is a beautiful woman who shows no discretion."

Knowing that it is important to take God's Word in totality and not isolation, I've come to summarize God's expectations of and opinions on beauty for my life as a believing woman: First, there is nothing sinful about physical beauty in itself. I can't find any verses in God's word that tell women to abstain from physical beauty; however, we read over and over again that outward appearance is *not* what is most important in life. Our character matters much more to God than our outer appearances. Lastly, we are not going to receive either eternal punishment or reward based on our outward looks. God looks at our hearts; He does not judge us as the world does. That should be a relief, instead of a restraint! *He created me.* He knows me intimately (Psalm 139:1-16). Beauty is not sinful, but it shouldn't be what consumes us. It is very easy to turn our priorities upside down and obsess about how we look rather than focus on who we are. Western culture lures us into idolizing a certain "look" and encourages us to employ tactics beyond what is reasonable or even healthy to gain that look. When our beauty desires become obsessive, motivating us to focus the majority of our time, energy, and extra money on our looks, we often end up neglecting our souls—and sometimes cause physical harm in our attempts to meet the world's standards.

CULTURAL INFLUENCES

It's easy for issues with our appearance to permeate our brains, steeping them in an astringent pickling juice of cultural expectations. Let's face it—women are thrown in the brine at a young age. Worldly standards of beauty drip from the shelves of retail stores and appear in our in-boxes as we grow older. We read magazines (or at least peep at the covers!) that immerse us in the downright confusing popular wisdom of the modern age:

- "Beware of eating disorders—but good luck finding cute clothes or keeping a media job if you're above a certain clothing size!"
- "Guard against date rape and sexual predators—but wear revealing and grown-up styles at young ages"

- "Celebrate your individuality—but watch TV shows and movies targeted at you where every single female is cookie-cutter trendy!"

These paradoxical messages are not verbalized, but they are hard to miss. Maybe that's why we cheer when we see a plus-sized actress or advertising model, or why tabloids try to catch famous women "without their make-up". Secretly, we all know that day to day reality is not always magazine cover beautiful for any of us. These are small cultural steps, but the real good news is found outside of Hollywood: whether the pervasive culture of beauty that surrounds us changes or not, the joyful message is that God *never* changes. He has always loved us for who we are — who He created us to be — and He always will. He looks at our insides, not our outsides. He fashioned us and we are important to him. He knows both the number of hairs on our heads (Matthew 10:30) and the motivation of our hearts (1Samuel 16:7). Beauty is fleeting, but God endures forever!

We all have different convictions about subjects that aren't laid out in black and white in God's Word. Some of us are convicted about things that others are not. Outer beauty and how we achieve it is no exception, and God works differently in people's lives to accomplish His purposes. I once heard a Christian author relate an anecdote related to the issue of God working differently in different lives. She shared that she had felt God calling her some time ago to experience a period of "fasting" from culture before speaking engagements. He had called her to separate herself from secular TV, music, and even things like shopping for a set period of time prior to the beginning of an event. She explained it was a specific calling on her life—a way for her to get "alone" with God and focus on Him and His Word. Once, while walking through an airport en route to one of these events, she saw an eye-catching blouse in the window of a shop. She considered buying it, despite her "fast" and, after pondering the decision, purchased it. This godly woman "wrestled" with God for a time after that decision—not because buying a blouse is a sin, but because He had specifically called on her to abstain. She repented of her blouse-buying, and relayed the somewhat humorous story of His conviction on her about it. Although we all laughed, we also acknowledged a grand reality: God may call one woman to stricter standards regarding her outward appearance than others, but that doesn't mean He condemns our attempt to look good.

I don't think God has an issue with haircuts, make-up or shopping—unless He has spoken specifically to us about it. In the same way, I don't think God has an issue with His children being attractive unless He has revealed to us that a particular behavior is a stumbling-block in our path. We must follow *God's* expectations for us. Culture would have urged to buy the blouse while we could find it. Culture would tell us we deserved it. Culture would remind us it was on sale! But we have to go with God when it comes to these issues. How much money, time, and energy we put into our physical appearance should depend on what God has impressed upon us. His Word is clear that if our desire for inner beauty is exceeded by our desire for outer gorgeousness, then we are making the world's expectations of beauty our idol, not living God's expectations for us.

POSSESSIONS

When I landed in West Africa in 1996—prepared for two years of missionary service in Bamako, Mali, I didn't know what to expect. I could only conjure up vague images from Feed the Children charity spots and occasional impressions from movies or a National Geographic special. I had been preparing myself for hot dry climates, primitive housing, and hungry people. I was ready to buckle down and learn a new language. I knew I would be overwhelmed, at first, by the differences between my own American culture and the West African one I was diving into. These expectations were met; I have many stories from Mali, some funny and some sad. But something I hadn't really expected stood out from all the other lessons I learned there—warm humanity and contentment can exist in the midst of abject poverty.

I quickly learned that West Africans are warm, hospitable, generous people. These families, who make on average $300-$400 a year, are always willing to help others in need. They may live in a one-room concrete-block house with no running water or electricity, but they will share a mat and a cool spot in the courtyard with a stranger who has no place to stay. They may have one meal to eat that day, but if someone hungry comes along he or she is welcome to sit down and eat from the family bowl. In addition to this generous spirit of hospitality is a strong will to live and a general positive attitude about life. In the two years I lived alongside some of the most financially-destitute people in the world, I learned what it truly meant to not make possessions my idols. These people who had very little in the way of material things seemed better off emotionally than many of us who are exponentially wealthy compared to them. It's not that Malian people never wanted to get ahead—many of them did, and others were striving for education so they *could* create more opportunity to achieve financial success. It was not the absence of money or possessions that made them more content, but the priorities in their lives that made them cheerful despite their poverty. I am convinced that they were the best teachers anyone could have of the truths laid out in Matthew 6:25: for, beyond not worrying about possessions, they had no lofty expectations of amassed wealth to interfere with their daily zest for the life set before them.

The Malians I knew lived life with warmth and openness. While their day-to-day tasks were all about survival, they also highly prioritized relationships. Time was not a matter to worry about—things happened when they happened! Malians loved being in the company of people while sharing stories, meals, and tea. Even those who looked to improve their lot were unencumbered by the driving force to "keep up with the Joneses." Malians were not ashamed of what they had or did not have; they never refrained from having guests over just because they lacked a great chair or a table. The Malians I knew—Christians and Muslims alike—were willing to get to know people and share their stories. They knew people weren't meant to be defined by the square-footage of their house, or mode of transportation. Nobody cared whether you owned a car, motor scooter, bicycle, or just walked, from point A to point B. Many Malians walked miles every day to attend both the Malian equivalent of a high school and an English language class. The cost of tuition wasn't as important as the work you put into learning. Education and knowledge were important, and Malians were patient about achieving them. Living in the midst of people who have almost nothing in the way of worldly things and surrounded by their culture, I experienced a shift in perspective and came to see the world very differently.

A MEMORY

I'm a better person because I lived in that African nation. I knew those people. I love them. I wish I could say that when I came back from my adventure abroad I followed the life lessons I learned from my Malian friends consistently. I *am* more convicted about investing time into people and relationships, but I still struggle to put it into practice. I *am* less enticed by the "bigger and better" mentality of America, but I still occasionally long to upgrade my house, car, and furniture. It's amazing how, despite our best efforts, we are continually seasoned by the cultural stew in which we daily swim. But any time I'm tempted to overlook the people in my life, or live above my means and spend frivolously, I reflect on my African memories and the desire passes away.

I remember sitting in a village, transparent green bugs biting into my skin. I was sitting between a shirtless little girl with tightly braided hair, yellowed from lack of nutrition, and a man with only one eye and a swollen hand so puffy that it had no bone definition, the fingers resembling a paw. I tuned in and out as a fellow missionary told the story of Cain and Abel in the Bambara language. My attention was drawn to a miniscule, and very dirty, kitten, mewing pitifully and weaving in and out of villagers' legs. Four men, six women, and roughly fifteen children were in the vicinity; half the population of the village of Baguinda. As my gaze moved from the hungry kitten to the dusty and scarred legs of the people sitting in the story circle, I was struck by a new reality. These people, who have little in the way of worldly possessions—one outfit, a few buckets, a mud brick hut, and maybe a single donkey or a bicycle for the entire community—were content. They were listening eagerly to the Bible story, and asking questions. They craved knowledge and human companionship, and thrived on conversation and relationship. The children were not disembodied faces once seen in a magazine, but real—breathing, wriggling, little bodies who smiled toothless grins at the visitors and greeted us with as much dignity as their village chiefs. They didn't see themselves as poor, suffering African children. They played, threw rocks at the chickens, and chased the baby goats in circles, peals of hilarious laughter ringing from the surrounding huts.

As my focus returned to the story of Cain and Abel and its denouement, the first drops of rain began to fall—the first since I'd arrived in West Africa at the height of the hot and dry season. As the first few raindrops touched my skin, I realized they were from the same God who sent thunderstorms across the Midwest and kept track of the hurricanes that blew across Florida. West Africa was just another crevice in the knuckles of the hands of the Almighty God, our Creator. As the drops fell more briskly, the Malians were hurriedly gathering the small wooden benches into a nearby hut. It was no bigger than an American bathroom, but we all crowded in to avoid the pouring rain. As we settled onto benches, children sprawling on the floor, the rain became hail, roaring on the makeshift tin roof with a deafening drum. It was pitch dark, so we left the door open. We were American and African, trying our best to communicate in one language, sitting knee-to-knee in the stifling heat in a hut that smelled of sweat and ground millet. We were cramped, we were hot, we were trapped by a hailstorm; but we were smiling, laughing, and realizing that humanity is the same at heart. We all craved relationship and compassion. We all desired laughter. We were all imperfect. Some of us had much, others had little—but we were all God's. His design from the beginning was for humans to be in relationship with Him and others as we partner together to work and live. Somehow, in the evolution of human existence and knowledge, many of us have lost touch with that original grand design. We have made life about *what* we want *when* we want it.

I think of this experience whenever I feel like my perspective needs to shift. In America, it is easy for us to become consumed with acquiring things instead of making time for people. We are expected to invest in our financial futures, our real estate, and our careers, but often fail to invest in people. There is nothing sinful about money, possessions, or jobs as long as they don't rule our choices. God's Word clearly states that the *love* of possessions is a root of all evil. It's all about priorities: God first, people second, and money somewhere after that. Paul found contentment "whether living in plenty or in want," and I learned that same lesson from the villagers of Baguinda. They were content to have each other, even when they had little else.

ROMANCE

When I was growing up, I eagerly anticipated *The Sound of Music*'s appearance in the nightly television line up every six months or so. As I tried to explain to my daughter a few weeks ago, when mommy was little there was no cable, no network devoted solely to children's programming, no DVRs; no Netflix™, no DVDs, and (in my family) not even a VCR until 1986. Therefore, it was a bright spot in my life when I again glimpsed the snowy mountaintop of the Austrian Alps and heard the first few symphonic chords of the tale of Maria. Her story, and her voice, always fascinated me. Has there ever been a better tale of a woman whose expectations were turned upside down? Perhaps one of the greatest quotes on expectations comes from a bit of wisdom the Reverend Mother passes along to Maria as she struggles to understand why her desire for a peaceful existence within the abbey walls is being rewritten by the very God who created her: "When God closes a door, somewhere He opens a window." As the all-knowing audience member I was after at least five viewings of the film (and later ten, fifteen, and even twenty), I wanted to tell Maria that her future as the wife of Captain Von Trapp and the mother of seven adoring children was far more appealing than her own choice of a celibate life in the strict convent surrounded by tattletale nuns who considered her only "a problem"!

While we may not end up hiking the Austrian Alps with Captain Von Trapp, we can all be assured that if we lay our expectations at God's feet and allow Him to shut our own self-serving doors, the windows He opens will be ones of freedom and fulfillment—however painful the process. Get ready for the raw emotion! This tale may make me sound like a love-sick idiot, but it is an important example of how our culture can manipulate women, and how we need to continue to seek God even if our initial expectations of love and romance aren't met. Much of my life has been devoted to teaching teenagers, and I can empathize with so many girls and young women when it comes to matters of the heart! A part of my former life was once very wounded by an unmet expectation.

"THE DESIRES OF YOUR HEART"

Although I grew up in an evangelical church and became a follower of Christ at age eight, I did not really understand a love relationship with Jesus until I was nineteen, when God spoke audibly to my heart and told me He loved me. Those of you who have encountered this deep experience with the Holy Spirit can testify that you *never* forget it. God's audible voice within you is unmistakable and makes such an impression that you have to work to miss it. I had been missing the core concept of God's overwhelming love for me. To finally be certain that the God of the universe knew me intimately, *saw* me, and *loved* me despite my faults was amazing and life-changing.

After this revelation, I finally dug into God's Word for myself, having relied on the opinions of pastors, Sunday School teachers, and youth leaders up to that point. A college friend of mine had a refrigerator magnet that read:

Delight yourself in the Lord and he will
give you the desires of your heart. -
Psalm 37:4

I had always been familiar with the verse—if you're churched, as I have been, you've heard it too (and probably seen it on any number of magnets, notebooks, prayer journals, and t-shirts). Despite the ubiquity of the verse, and all the merchandise bearing it, there are many who do not "get" the meaning of it. I was one of them. At the age of nineteen, dreaming of my very own cinematic love story—sans the seven children—I began to interpret the verse somewhat differently: if you follow Jesus whole-heartedly, He will give you what you want. What I wanted was to find my own Captain von Trapp—that mythical man who is changed by a woman's love and is completely devoted to her. Enter my all-consuming expectation in the spring of 1992: Mason Duncan. *

THE FAIRYTALE OF THE MIND

I had been in love with Jesus for about ten months when I first noticed Mason. I was a sophomore in college, involved in an active student ministry, active in a local church, and feeling like I was truly following Christ for the first time, when I spotted Mason in a literature class. His blue eyes made my knees weak and his voice tingled along

---

*Names in this story have been changed to protect the innocent.

my spine—but he had no idea who I was. I didn't really know who he was either, just how he looked and, let's be honest, even single ladies who love the Lord are not above sheer physical attraction to a good-looking man.

As my junior year began, I was pleasantly surprised (who am I kidding—*ecstatic!*) to find Mason in two of my classes. "What are the odds that this would happen at my large university?" I thought to myself. "It *must* be God's hand!" Unfortunately, I didn't just *think* those things, I began to *say* them to my roommate and friends. I also began to dream and dwell—those dangerous "D"s. My brain quickly became a cozy space for romantic musings about Mason. They took up full residence in the part of my mind reserved for down-time and day-dreaming. Dwelling on something builds a stronghold, whether for good or evil. And speaking things aloud can make us stronger in our pursuit of God, or dissuade us. The more we verbalize an idea, or dwell on it in our brains, the more we begin to validate, justify, and grow that idea into reality. We play around with it, we embellish it, we let it roost. I can say with some confidence that I'm not the only woman to ever be in this coop.

To my delight, Mason and I were soon paired up by one of our professors for a class project. I learned that he was not only gorgeous, but an intelligent student and, most of all, a believer. Perhaps this really was my very own Captain Von Trapp—minus that annoying whistle! I prayed *every night* that Mason Duncan would be the one

God had for me. Remember Psalms 37:4? I was convinced that since Mason was the "desire of my heart," God would answer my prayers. According to all the movies I'd ever seen, I deserved this fairy tale to come true: "Girl meets gorgeous boy, who is also a great person; girl falls in love and boy falls in love back—even if it takes boy longer than girl to realize it." But watching fairy tale romances and being in love with Jesus are no certain shield against the heartache of unrequited love.

As the year wore on, Mason and I saw each other more frequently, chiefly because I began to manipulate my schedule to "run into" him. I knew God meant for us to be together, but it couldn't hurt to give Him a little help. Surely if I spent more time with Mason he would drop that long-distance girlfriend he sometimes talked about and fall in love with me. I saved Mason's messages on my answering machine—the old kind, with the cassette tapes—when he called about school. I was always willing to drop everything to help him with some paper or class assignment. We spent four weeks together in the summer term. He took me out for my twenty-first birthday and told me he was seriously contemplating breaking up with his girlfriend. How my heart beat with anticipation at that prospect! Then he left, and I didn't see him or hear from him again for many weeks. Until...

One Wednesday evening in the early fall of my senior year, I dropped by the student center to grab dinner before Bible study. Suddenly, I heard *that* voice say my name. I had run into him unexpectedly a few times since the semester had begun, but we had no classes together and he hadn't made an effort to spend time with me. I turned to see Mason—sitting at a table with a petite, blonde-haired girl. My heart dropped like an elevator car with a cut cable. I *knew*. I knew the second I turned around, before any other words came out of his mouth, before he introduced me to Anne Olivia Payton*, I knew. God's still small voice spoke into my heart and mind. *"He's going to marry her."*

It was only God's grace that allowed me to plaster a smile on my face, tell her it was nice to meet her, apologize for having to run, and jet from the student center, down the steps, and to my car with tears streaming down my face. By the time I reached it, I was crying so hard I couldn't see to unlock the door; I haphazardly threw my things, food included, into the car. I sat in the driver's seat for twenty minutes, sobbing as if the world were ending. *"Why*, God?? What happened to the desires of my heart? I expected you to come through! I'm following you! I'm studying your Word! I'm living for you! I'm not having premarital sex! I'm going on mission trips! I'm leading a discipleship group! WHY NOT ME?!?" I beat the steering wheel, my eyes swollen, my heart broken, my stomach turning over. It hurt like no other emotional hurt I had ever experienced. I had had crushes before, but this was the first time I had really trusted God to meet my expectations. Although I didn't realize it until much later — when I was less emotionally charged and able to think clearly — my pursuit of Mason had elevated him to idol status in my life.

The following spring I was lining up for my graduation ceremony when Mason and Anne Olivia yelled out a greeting to me. I hadn't encountered either one of them in many months, in fact I lived to *avoid* them but here they were, smiling at me like I was as deliriously happy as they were. We hadn't exchanged a word since that awful night, and I was still too deeply hurt to converse normally—I said a quick hello but I couldn't stand with them and contain my tears for more than a few minutes. In the presence of both of them, my heart was still raw.

Part of me still felt betrayed and rejected by God, not just Mason. However, because God kept leading me with cords of kindness and love and grace, I never stopped serving Him. By that graduation day I had already started the process of becoming a Journeyman: a short-term missionary. I continued to focus my energy on that; praying, filling out mountains of paperwork, living with my parents, and working all summer to save money. I got my overseas assignment—Mali, West Africa, which had been the desire of my heart. I made new friends who shared my heart for missions, and I began to see God's future for me, at least for the next two years. I was slowly beginning to heal from the disappointment of my own expectations and focus on God's expectations for me.

Those two years in West Africa were a sweet time for my relationship with my Creator. They weren't easy by any stretch, but I had time for reflection. I realized that I had held onto my expectations that Mason and I would end up married so tightly, that I had almost worshipped him. I had put the fairy tale ending on the altar of my mind and thrown all of my emotional energy at it. I had been obsessed with anticipation, and idolized those feelings. I realized that Mason had *never* been God's desire for me. If I had married Mason, I wouldn't have ended up in Africa, and that was exactly where God wanted me. I won't lie and say it didn't hurt anymore. When my college roommate wrote that Mason and Anne Olivia had been married, I shed tears of nostalgia, remorse, and defeat. I knew part of my pain was wounded pride. *I* hadn't been chosen. She had. It would have been easy to wallow in self-pity, but God had put me in the heart of a third-world country for a reason. I began to grow stronger—not more confident in my looks or prospects for a romantic relationship—but stronger in who I was in Christ. God taught me lessons about faith and trust in Him that I couldn't have learned any other way. He was developing an identity for me in Him. God used that time with a people full of life, living simply, to teach me the benefit of not always wanting more. He separated me irrevocably from Mason to show me the dichotomy of desires and true need and contentment. He used that time to make me stronger.

Seven years later, God decided I was ready to learn what it means to be truly loved by a man. I have never doubted my husband's love for me. I never had to manipulate situations or pursue him, obsess over him or discuss details with friends. In fact, I cannot remember a single time in a year of dating and over a decade of marriage when I have not been assured that my husband loved me. Whether I have been sick or healthy, moody or tranquil, working for a salary or working at home, he has never given me a reason to doubt that he loves me just the same. If someone had told the heartbroken girl who cried for Mason that she would love, and be loved, securely by a man she probably would not have believed it. Like Maria in her convent, she didn't know what to expect, but God had plans for her all along.

Chapter 3
Expectations of Faith

EMOTIONAL EXCITEMENT

In a news interview recently, a musician stated, "nothing is as spiritual as performing live." It wasn't the first time I'd heard this assertion: actors, musicians, dancers—even athletes—have characterized a performance as spiritual. While performing well in front of an audience and being applauded and praised *does* create an emotional high, it's not "spiritual." Our culture has confused emotionalism with spirituality and, because of this, we are misled and deceived. When emotions become our gauge of spirituality, we walk down the path of disillusionment and begin to think that a spiritual connection with God requires some sort of heightened emotional reaction. Conversely, we begin to see any emotional reaction as a spiritual message or sign.

Any performance or feat that makes us stop and say, "Darn, I'm good!" is *not* spiritual. That reaction means we are focused on self. That doesn't mean that achieving goals and feeling good about it is wrong—emotional highs are fun! Doing something really well and getting accolades creates endorphins, which are good. The danger lies in judging the "spirituality" of an experience based solely on our emotional reaction; it is easy to idolize that emotional high and, consequently, fall into a pattern of simply seeking positive emotions instead of seeking God.

We are often misled in our relationship with God because we base decisions about serving Him on our emotions. We choose a church based on our emotional reaction to the pastor or worship band, or how we feel when we walk in the door. We treat other people in direct proportion to the emotions they evoke. That's the great divide, the culture clash. The world teaches us to focus on ourselves and do what makes us happy; we can ignore people who don't make us happy, who annoy us, or who don't meet our every need. Conversely, our spiritual God commands us to love, pray for, and forgive people, regardless of the emotions they evoke. That doesn't mean we have to be best friends with someone who grates on our nerves, or buddy up with someone whose values and life goals oppose our own; however, there is a level of respect that we are required to show people for the simple reason that God created *all* of humanity in His image. It's a command that does not take our personal happiness into account. God often calls us into an emotionally tough situation to do His will, and we have to separate our emotions from the task in order to be effective. That's spiritual too because we are obeying the conviction of His Holy Spirit

What if Christ had acted on emotions when faced with his arrest and murder on the cross? In his humanity He didn't *want* to do it. He prayed that God would "take this cup" from him, but He followed through with God's will because it *was* God's will—not because it made him feel good. And it's a good thing He did: the crucifixion and resurrection was part of God working all things together for the "good for those who love him and have been called according to his purpose" (Romans 8:28). We would be utterly without hope had Jesus regarded his emotions as a spiritual register and had not paid the penalty of death for our sins. Jesus could have lived by the emotional highs of accolades He received for performing miracles. He could have listened to the mocking crowd and in an act of glorious "in your face", come down from the cross in an amazing display. It would have been easy for Him to worship His own power and deny the cross were it not for the love he had for people, even those who hated Him. That was spiritual.

BIBLICAL SPIRITUALITY

We're human. We are emotional creatures. I will be the first to admit that I relish a good emotional experience. Certain songs flowing from the radio can make me feel happy and glowing inside because of the message or memory attached. Belly laughs seem to heal hurts in me and a movie like *Les Miserables* with great acting, exceptional music, and a profoundly symbolic and redeeming story makes me cry and fills me with a passionate love. And while I firmly believe God can and does speak to us in the midst of emotional experiences, none of the aforementioned experiences in themselves are spiritual ones. Look at Paul's life to sort out this complicated relationship between emotion and true spirituality. During the Apostle's ministry he argued for Christ, sometimes with a logical and analytical mind and other times with a heart full of emotion. But whether steeped in emotion or separated from it, he was more in tune with the Holy Spirit, more "spiritual" than the majority of his contemporaries. It wasn't Paul's emotion that separated him from the crowd, it was his devotion to God and his unwavering faith that Jesus Christ was exactly who He said he was. Paul lived for Christ despite his circumstances. Imprisoned and in chains, he prayed and sang hymns with Silas until they were released from their cells by an earthquake from the Lord. Instead of running out in a state of emotional euphoria or self-aggrandizement, Paul and Silas remained in their cells, as did the other prisoners, to spare the life of the jailer (Acts 16:25-34). In Acts 27, Paul, bound for Rome as a prisoner, warned the ship's crew that they should stay in port for the winter or else they would suffer great loss. They didn't listen and were blown off course in a storm. They lost all of their supplies and the ship itself but, thanks to Paul's prayers, not their lives. These are two examples that display Paul's level-headedness in what were seemingly highly charged emotional situations. In other areas of his ministry, such as his letters to Timothy, we see an emotional apostle—one

66

who is wrenched with his feelings for unbelieving fellow Jews and stubborn Gentiles.

When the twelve apostles gathered after Jesus's ascension and were consumed by the Holy Spirit, speaking in foreign languages so that everyone present understood what was being said in his or her own language (Acts 2)—*that* was a "spiritual" moment. It was literally full of God's spirit! Some observers reacted emotionally while others didn't; many marveled while others cynically assumed the apostles were drunk. Neither emotion—the marvel or the cynicism—changed God's power. The emotions, or lack thereof, did not alter the influence of His Holy Spirit that led many to be saved.

It was "spiritual" when Jesus healed a paralytic and told him to take up his mat and walk (Mark 2:1-12). The paralytic reacted with joy and emotion, but Jesus remained calm. However, when He saw the raw emotion and grief after Lazarus's death, He reacted in a deeply emotional manner before praying for God's Spirit to raise his friend (John 11). Jesus's experiences with the paralytic and with Lazarus were both "spiritual", not because of their emotional content but because the Spirit of God was moving and working through them.

My favorite Christian singer-songwriter of all time, Rich Mullins, once said in a radio interview that being spiritual was taking a meal to a neighbor or mowing the lawn for someone who couldn't do it themselves. Basically his view was any time we act unselfishly in the service and best interest of others, doing the things God has commanded—however mundane they may seem—we are spiritually motivated. It can be anything that God has ordained and convicted us to do by His Spirit, from the simplest daily task to the most difficult, seemingly insurmountable one. The presence of the Holy Spirit (and our response to Him) is what prompts us to grow on a spiritual level, not emotional highs received from performances and the accolades of adoring crowds.

THE PURSUIT OF HAPPINESS

Not only can we not idolize emotional reactions as spiritual; more specifically, happiness in itself is not necessarily a spiritual marker. How many times have we heard "Do what makes you happy" or a parent say, "All I've ever wanted is for my children to be happy?" Out of all emotions, the Western world holds happiness in highest regard. We have been culturally conditioned to believe that immediate change is needed if we are experiencing *any* unhappiness—even if that "change" is against God's will. Happiness, when it is our ultimate goal, can also become our ultimate idol. Peace, joy, and contentment outweigh it, because happiness is a come-and-go emotion. What makes us happy one day may not make us happy the next, so the pursuit of happiness is a dangerous thing. We become like a pendulum, swinging wildly to and fro to keep our happy feelling.

People who seek constant happiness, devoid of Christ, resort to any means necessary to sustain the emotion, and often engage in detrimental behaviors at the expense of themselves and others to achieve what they "feel" is happiness: adulterous relationships, excessive shopping, binge eating, drug addiction, alcohol abuse, even risky foolishness like teenage car-surfing are experiences that create a rush of adrenaline or a drug-induced euphoria, but the high can just as quickly turn to despair. We justify bad decisions by saying they "make us happy" and expect our choices to make us feel good. When they don't, we look for something else to fill our happiness tank. Sheryl Crow may not be a theologian, but she nails our cultural contradiction when she sings, "If it makes you happy, it can't be that bad. If it makes you happy, why the h#@! are you so sad?"*

It is shocking to realize that we will be more in tune with the spirit of God if we aren't always happy. Enduring times of sadness and loneliness, or just neutrality, while maintaining our convictions grows us much stronger than the scramble to maintain euphoria. Don't get me wrong—this doesn't mean we're *never* supposed to be happy. It doesn't even mean that happiness is bad. In fact, happiness is pretty great. The problem exists when we sacrifice our values, identity, or the people we love to gain "happiness".

One of the toughest lessons on the road to spiritual maturity is that God is not *nearly* as concerned

*Sheryl Crow. "If it Makes You Happy." *Sheryl Crow*. 1996. A&M.

with our happiness as with our wholeness, growth, devotion, and salvation. It's not that God doesn't want us to be happy; it just isn't at the top of His priority list. He would rather me be content in my circumstances as long as I am in His will. He will not negate His precepts or ignore bad behavior just for me to achieve a level of "happiness." If you don't believe me, just try to find one person from God's Word—Genesis through Revelation—who was happy all the time. You can't do it because it's impossible! Abraham gave up a lot of security to follow God and, while he was blessed beyond measure, he still had struggles (Genesis 16). David was chosen as King of Israel, yet found that even power and wealth couldn't make him happy all of the time; he sought out pleasure with the consequence of despair (2 Samuel 12 and Psalm 42). Even Solomon—the richest man in the world—was visited by bouts of depression. Just read Ecclesiastes. Humans will not be happy 100% of the time. Knowing you aren't expected to be happy all of the time—but are, rather, called to be content with where God has you at the moment—is liberating. Trusting in God and worshipping Him is a divine joy that trumps idolizing a constant state of happiness.

SPIRITUAL MOUNTAINTOPS

Life is not without valleys (Psalm 23). We will face opposition (Matthew 5). These are truths from God's Word. God has plans to prosper us and not to harm us—plans to give us a hope and a future.

(Jeremiah 29:11) God works all things together for good for those who love Him and are called according to His purpose. (Romans 8:28) These are also truths from God's Word. They are evident in the stories of believers who have gone before, like Joseph, Job, and Paul, even Jesus himself. These four men in particular faced great opposition and spent time in valleys of faith that would have crushed many of us. However, as we look at the intricately woven fabric of their lives, we see the tremendous blessings of God in all of them. They trusted God in the midst of their valleys, but their trust didn't exclude fear, frustration, and grief.

It's funny how vision is limited when you're in a valley. If you've ever hiked to the bottom of the Grand Canyon (or even a smaller crevasse) you know that, suddenly, you can see only what is to your right or left. Your distance-vision is eradicated. In the Appalachians in the Eastern United States, the hours of sunlight in the valleys are greatly diminished from those received by people on the "other side of the mountain." Valleys lessen our light and obstruct our vision. When we're in the midst of life's valleys—an illness, a time of depression, the death of someone we love, a lost job, or a time of financial strain—it's easy to despair because we can't see very far ahead and feel surrounded by darkness. These are the times when Christ is speaking to us to be still, to listen to His voice, and to trust that He is in control. This is no easy task.

Perhaps as Christians this is the area where we are most unprepared. We don't want to hear about valleys; we want to ignore opposition, trouble, and the reality of Satan roaming the earth "seeking whom he may devour" (1Peter 5:8). In my mind, I would much rather live perpetually on the mountaintop. I am thin-skinned and troubled by opposition. Like any control freak, I like to take charge and "see" a way out of every situation. When I can't, I feel panicky. The reality I'm facing is that sometimes I have to accept God's grace to live in the valley, and just be patient until He delivers me. I have to walk through experiences where only *He* can be in control. It's scary. There is a reason God continually punctuates the appearances of heavenly beings with the command to "Fear not!" Those glimpsing the physical presence of divine beings were found shaking in their shoes. When we *see* the spiritual plane—even if only for a moment—we are suddenly gripped with the fear of God and the knowledge of the larger battle being waged.

GRIEF AND SORROW

Our culture chases after a feel-good spirituality of constant happiness and prosperity. As believers, we also want to hear that following Christ will be an easy endeavor *all* of the time; a utopia without struggles, obstacles, and setbacks. We live in an era when a "prosperity gospel" mentality is rampant. Yet I have never run across a verse in God's Word that promises obstacle-free, perpetual happiness and prosperity to people who live a life of faith. God *does* say He has plans to prosper us and not harm us; plans to give us a hope and a future. He does not say anywhere exactly what our prosperity will look like, nor that it will be continual. Our tendencies toward financial prosperity and living in a state of comfort subject us all to two major pitfalls: equating our faith-level to our circumstances (believing they exist in a state of precariously balanced equilibrium) and believing that grief and sorrow could not possibly be part of the divine Christian experience.

Look again at four Biblical examples of men who eventually prospered in different ways, but who also went through dark valleys to get there. Joseph endured slavery and imprisonment before becoming the most powerful and wealthy man in Egypt. Job lost everything—his family, his health, and his riches—only to regain them tenfold because he never lost his faith. Paul faced many hardships and rejections, but the letters he wrote became the spinal cord of Christian life and part of God's Word forever. Jesus endured humiliation, rejection, and death, but ultimately conquered sin and death to create the opportunity for us all to inherit eternal life! The lives of these men prove that God's ways are not like our own and that, if we adhere too strongly to our own expectations for our lives, we may miss God's opportunities and blessings.

The love, joy, peace, patience, kindness, goodness, gentleness, faithfulness, and self-control that

God describes as the fruit of the Holy Spirit (Galatians 5:22-23) are blessings that stem from trust in Christ—the knowledge that He is in control, not us. Just because Christ is working in us doesn't mean we will be exempt from outer struggles, temptations, troubles, grief, or sorrow. Because we have expectations that our lives will be rosy, and because we live in a society that profits from selling us comfort, we can feel disillusioned if something goes wrong and our hopes go unfulfilled. We may have months, even years, when the path we're on doesn't make sense to others. But we know we're on the path God has marked for us. We may endure painful things but God has a clearer vision; He sees how we are connected to others in ways we cannot when our view is obstructed in the valley.

SADIE

My dear friend, Amber, and her husband Tim walk in the midst of a pretty deep valley. Their toddler daughter was diagnosed with a rare, acute myeloma leukemia in the Fall of 2012. The doctors caught it early and treated it aggressively, but little Sadie suffered seizures, strokes, and partial paralysis as a result of this disease's attacks on her little body. Amber shared during the beginning of the journey in her online journal:

So, despite the fact that it is absolutely heart-wrenching to watch our precious child have to undergo aggressive chemotherapy to fight this terrible disease, could it be that we should feel honored that God is using us and our experience to draw people closer to Him? I honestly don't feel like God is punishing us or that He has removed His protective hand from our family. But I DO feel that His purpose is much bigger than keeping me comfortable and happy all the time. Maybe, just maybe, He is allowing this to happen in our family because there is someone somewhere who needs to watch this unfold so that they can see His glory and put their trust in Him. Someone like me. I am a believer and I am not ashamed of my faith, but that faith has never been put to the test like it is in my life right now.

I have no option but to put this situation in God's hands, and to try to trust that He will not leave me or forsake me. That He loves me and is not trying to destroy me or my family. He is actually drawing us closer together, and closer to Him. This is easier said than done. And for those of you who have mentioned my strength...I am telling you that it is not MY strength. This is strength that can only come from the Lord. This is the

*hardest thing I have ever experienced,
and I honestly am taking this moment
by moment. The big picture is too overwhelming ...* *

Amber's candor, transparency, and trust in
Jesus never faded during the battle for Sadie's life.
Jesus took Sadie home to be with Him on Decem-
ber 21, 2012, exactly 40 days after they began to
fight for her life. While I trust God's decision, it is
so difficult to process this, even now, through the
shock and grief. Questions keep filling my mind.
Why Sadie? Why these godly parents and friends?
Why now? I don't have answers.

The inexplicable things of life—the heart-
wrenching tragedies and struggles—are not short
journeys we can travel with our own strength.
Even though trusting God means often *not* knowing the answer to "why", God doesn't love us any
less for asking. After Job's catastrophic losses; the
attempts of his friends to convince him it must
be a burning sin in his own life that caused his
tragedy; and Job's cries of mourning, confusion,
and despair to God — God not only heard Job,
and reminded Job that He, God, was and is and
will be in control, Yahweh Adonai also completely
restored Job's life. God is in the business of never
leaving His children. God is in the business of

*Amber Davis. "Lessons Learned and Other Heartfelt Ram-
blings." Accessed November 27, 2012. www:caringbridge.org/
visit/sadiedavis/jounal

healing and restoration. While journeying in valleys of grief, despair, or heartbrokenness, we are able to live without fear of evil because God walks with us — His shepherding tools — the rod to protect us and the staff to rescue us are ever present. He gives us rest and sustenance when we need it. He brings us peace in our darkest hours. (Psalm 23) And He knows. Jehovah Jireh, Adonnai, who clothed Himself with mortality and limited himself to the natural confines of earth, who experienced torturous death and who sacrificed for us, knows. These valley journeys present us with two paths. One requires us to continue to trust and follow God, to grieve with hope, to mourn loss but know we will see those we love again. The other path is to harden our hearts to God because we don't understand and aren't in control of all the circumstances of our lives.

Two of the biggest misconceptions non-Christians have of believers are that our trust in God means we don't grieve loss, and that we are senseless to trust in a God that allows things like the death of a child, or the genocide of a race of people, or the splitting apart of a church. My response is that grief is a natural part of life and in no way separates us from Christ, who himself experienced grief as He walked the earth. Second, God allows us freewill as He did from the beginning. With Adam and Eve's choices, sin and death entered the world. It is not a pretty reality, but it is also not one God keeps secret. (Romans 5:12-21) Although I cannot begin to wrap my brain around all of the pain and suffering that exist in this world, I also cannot begin to wrap my brain around the width and height and depth of the love of Christ for us. I will hold tightly to Christ because He holds tightly to me. Whether I laugh or cry, obey or sin, He never lets go. Paul reminds me, "If God is for [me] who can be against [me]? He did not even spare his own Son, but offered him up for us all; how will he not also with Him grant us everything? . . . Who can separate us from the love of Christ? Can affliction or anguish or persecution or famine or nakedness or danger or sword? . . . No in all these things we are MORE than victorious." (Romans 8:31-32, 35, 37)

Back to my dear friend, Amber and her faith in the midst of grief, questioning, and anguish of heart over the separation from her little girl. The most difficult and trying experience of her life and her husband's life is not over, but their transparent walk inspires many to faith. While Amber and Tim are perfect examples of what it means to trust God without reserve, they would be the first to admit *they* aren't "perfect." That's the point. They are *real*. At Sadie's funeral, God gave Tim the grace and strength to stand and challenge us with both their heartbreak and their unwavering faith. It was a heart-shattering testimony to God's Lordship amidst sorrow and God's sustaining love that guards against bottomless despair. Tim and Amber exhibit that quality that so many of us lack—the ability to be totally out of control of a situation and still be completely in love with Jesus. Even almost a year after Sadie went to be with the Lord, the path is still thick with grief, sorrow, and anguish, but it is also full of joy, blessings, and healing. Contrary to our current culture's perspective, these are not mutually exclusive experiences.

Not all of us are tested in our faith to the bone-depths that Tim and Amber were, but we are all in the mix of the world, earthly life, and humanity. Our earthly bodies experience rips, tears, and fading but those in Christ will someday be clothed in eternal bodies that match our spirits and souls, that reveal the driving life-force within us all. The grace of God enables us to have eternity, and Jesus's sacrifice on the cross triumphed over death. Once we are God's children, "I am persuaded that not even death or life, angels or rulers, things present or things to come, hostile powers, height or depth, or any other created thing will have the power to separate us from the love of God that is in Christ Jesus our Lord." (Romans 8:38-39)

TAMMY AND DREW

In Chapter One, I mentioned an old hymn that speaks strongly to me "The Solid Rock." A stanza of it jumps out at me as I ponder and pray for my dear friends who have experienced loss: "When darkness veils His lovely face, I rest on His unchanging grace; in every high and stormy gale, my anchor holds within the veil.*" These words remind me of my friends Tim and Amber. They

*Edward Mote. "Solid Rock." *Hymns of Praise*. 1836.

also remind me of my college friend Tammy, who lost her husband.

Drew was the love of Tammy's life since college and together they parented two children. They never stopped praising, trusting, or serving God throughout Drew's battle with cancer, even when they knew he was going to die. His earthly body is gone now, but Drew's spirit lives on. His testimony, his faith, his example and those of his wife, Tammy, are still a testimony. I admire the complete transparency in Tammy's blog posts about dealing with Drew's death—she never conceals the pain, or denies the joys that still occur. She still experiences sadness, occasional anger, and even days when she doesn't feel like getting out of bed, but her faith lives on. To say that faith requires an absence of emotion is as much of a lie as saying faith equals emotion.

In *The Gift of Imperfection*, researcher and psychologist Brené Brown says, "We cannot selectively numb emotions. When we numb the painful emotions, we also numb the positive emotions."* I thought of Amber and Tim and Tammy when I read this. They aren't trying to numb their grief. They are brave enough to feel the pain and, in doing so, also feel the joy that still exists in life. Because for those in Christ, there is still joy — in the midst of sorrow, heartache, and a valley road. God's children are anchored to truth in the

*Brené Brown. *The Gift of Imperfection*. (Center City, MN: Hazelden, 2010), 70

midst of the storm. Though their ship can be tossed, it cannot be lost.

SPIRITUAL ATTACK

I don't like to think about spiritual warfare, or God's permissive will that allows Satan to attack and wreak havoc in people's lives. I want to pretend it doesn't exist. It's hard to accept that God allows bad things to happen — but as a result of our freewill and Satan's attempts to deceive us– they do. I was recently forced to take a hard look at the issue when a form of spiritual attack began manifesting itself in my life.

In a recent season of my life, I began experiencing days of panic and depression. Although I knew in my heart that God was in control, that He loved me, and that He had not left me, my mind was doing its best to convince me otherwise. I had never experienced anything like this before. These hours of attack filled me with hopelessness and fear. As I called out to God, He brought me a modicum of comfort, but the attacks didn't lift completely for months. While these dark periods could have been caused in part by the circumstances of my life, I *knew* the attacks were spiritual in nature. God prompted me one day, in the midst of an hour of panic and darkness, to contact a mentor of mine whom I had not seen in a long time. She prayed over me and spoke scripture and truth to me, reminding me that God was in control and that facing opposition was part of living in a troubled world. I thank God that He provided this sister to give me comfort and hope in the midst of the storm. I was reminded that God always knows what we need in times of spiritual warfare. He knows that sometimes we need to feel a hug, hear words of encouragement, or feel the warmth of a hot cup of tea prepared by a supportive friend. Although He sent this mentor to me at a specific time, with a specific purpose, and her prayers DID help, it was not as if the despair lifted like a rain cloud. I battled it for some time after that. I cannot pinpoint a day or an hour when God removed it, but I know now that it is gone. I refused to let go of what I knew was truth despite the way I *felt*.

Not every believer who is making a difference for God faces circumstances that bring heart-wrenching grief, but we all experience times of emotional panic or depression to some degree. Many don't experience obvious attacks—maybe that's what leads us to question *why* when we are suffering (or not suffering) the side effects of spiritual warfare and stuck in a valley. While the "whys" may never be answered in this life, it is human nature for us to desire an answer—a reason behind every circumstance. Our desire to know this "why" when it comes to the spiritual side of our lives creates emotional reactions: guilt (blaming our own actions or lack thereof for causing us to walk in a valley); anger (blaming God for devastating us); disconnection (living in a state of denial by covering our emotions with excessive behavior); debilitating grief (mourning our losses to the point where it devastates our day-to-day lives). In these valleys, when we cannot see far ahead, the truths of God often escape us. But just as in a physical valley, we can look up to see the light, in the valleys of our lives, we can look up to God. Not physically up. Although God created the skies, the stars, the moon, the sun, he does not physically live there. He is not a mythical creature sitting atop a cloud holding a harp, but He is "high above us". He is above us in knowledge, in power, in love. We look "up" to His perfection and rest in His grace.

Being high above us, in knowledge and power, God is in no way surprised or offended by our emotions — he created them. Second, He is still in control, whatever the circumstances. Third, neither those circumstances, nor our emotions about them, are an accurate gauge of God's love for us or our love for Him. God knows us intimately and He has a plan beyond our ability to fathom. He promises that He will never give us more temptation than we can endure and that He will always provide a way out. (1 Corinthians 10:13) That means even in our temptation to despair, to give up, or to stop following, God will provide a way for us to reach out to Him, past our emotions, and grab hold. Raw emotion is a natural human response to death, separation, divorce, despairing thoughts, or even financial turmoil; but our emotions only become idols when they—rather than God—begin to rule our decisions and our lives.

One would expect the arms of the church to be one of the safest places on earth. After all, a church building's main area of worship is traditionally called the "sanctuary"—a holy and peaceful place set apart for God. While the New Testament tells us that, as believers, *we* are the temple of the Holy Spirit (1 Corinthians 3:16-17), we still think of these man-made structures as the center of God's presence. This leads us to idolize a building just like we do other "stuff."

In fact for most people, the word "church" immediately conjures up images of structures; a hallowed sunlit spot in a small country church pew, or a conclave or station of the cross in a candle-lit Catholic Cathedral. For others, "church" speaks of an event. Church is something they *do*. The word represents motions and routines: Sunday School, worship services, scripture reading, prayers, candle lighting, and Communion. There is nothing wrong with finding moments of rest and peace in a building designed with the intent to bring glory to God. Nor is there harm in the routines of worship developed by various denominations of believers. But let's be honest—the original framework for the church established in the New Testament was a framework of *people*. (Acts 2) When the buildings, structures, or routines of "church" tend to overshadow the relationships of the people who make up a congregation, threatening to weaken or destroy what should be their bonds of love, then those structures or routines have become our idols.

God calls on us to make church an inclusive place, one that welcomes any wounded person into God's loving arms and commits to disciplining new believers in His Word. When we narrow our definition of "church" to mere buildings, we often don't invite others in. When our framework is built on nothing more than programs and events, our expectations for church growth will eventually drop off. Faulty programming or the expense of running massive church buildings can make a congregation crabby, and the process of "de-programming" can be equally as messy. In fact, the selfish wish to control what church is can bring a church family to its knees.

THE BODY OF CHRIST

Internal conflict will show whether your church is spiritually built on rock or sand. Because of disagreements over programming, worship style, "space," and authority, my former church family was washed into the tide. It is difficult to describe the ripping apart, both inside and out, that is the destruction of a body of Christ to someone who has not experienced it. A casual observer, an un-invested bystander, may escape this process unscathed. But for those with deep roots in a body of believers—who have invested time, love, and relationship to the congregation—it is like a devastating divorce. The pain is intense and seems endless, sharpening with every small decision made within the church family. Times of discord are when we, as believers, must choose to follow God's lead and build our foundation on His rock, or put ourselves in control and founder in the sand.

This once dear church was where my husband and I had met, grown spiritually, and served together. The place held many fond memories, both spiritual, and familial, comforting, and familiar. The pastor's passion for outreach had led my husband to Christ. Our wedding ceremony was held in the sanctuary, our babies dedicated there. Our pastor's wife was a quiet picture of wisdom, grace, and compassion. I served on a mission trip with one of their children. I loved and respected this family.

As I watched the body of Christ I thought I knew unraveling, I couldn't understand how a group of people who professed to be believers could hone in on one specific and devilish purpose: to tear each other, and a body of Christ, apart. I was dumbfounded by the hateful words and actions spewed in the form of "righteous indignation." When our pastor eventually resigned and moved away—under much conflict and pressure from some members of the church—it broke my heart. I remember thinking to myself, "*This* is what a true broken heart feels like." It was nothing like my experience in college when Mason Duncan found someone else to marry. This was a different kind of heartbreak—a deep, true sorrow for everyone involved, from my pastor to the church staff and, ultimately, my greater church family. It was not a heartache that ended suddenly, and in fact, still pops up at times when I'm feeling reminiscent and in a mood to be melancholy. Ripping apart the body of Christ is always tearing apart what was meant to work in harmony; family being peeled away, bit by bit.

Time passed. Staff came and went. After so much finger-pointing and false accusation, some leaders bowed out gracefully; others "separated" themselves from the conflict in a state of denial. Finally, my husband and I—who had stayed faithful through so many changes and tried to be respectful of elders and give the benefit of the doubt to those with seemingly good intentions—felt God was giving us the freedom to leave. We chose a different group of believers in which to invest our time. Like us, most of our church family did not lose faith in God because of those trials, but it would be a lie to say that none of them did or that it didn't affect us at all. Because our foundation was built ultimately on God (and He sure hadn't changed!), we were able to move on and become involved in another church body. But we were not emotionally immune. I didn't realize how emotional I still was until I saw my former pastor and his wife in a surprise reunion—after over two years. I cannot describe the emotions that washed over me when I embraced them after that long separation. I have respect and gratitude for their leadership and grace. While seeing them was emotional—and it felt *great* to give them a hug—I realized I was already part of a new body, and I was okay with that. While I loved my former pastor and his family, they were not God to me, just dearly loved people. And all of us imperfect people who love each other still cannot equal one perfect God.

God lends us resilience, even in the most devastating circumstances. When our expectations are not met or an unexpected blow crushes us, we keep going—even if we are dazed by grief or shock and simply going through the motions. Although my exterior grew a shell of resiliency after we watched our church destroy itself, the grief never fully went away until I saw our pastor and his wife again. God gently reminded me that He has provided me with a new church family and, while I will always miss those wonderful people, He has been faithful to take care of them too.

GOD'S PURPOSES

I could never have known in the "heyday" of that church family that it would end so harshly. My views and expectations of "church" will never be quite the same. I'm pretty sure that was one of God's purposes. In more than one place in scripture, God scattered believers to spread His Gospel. God is the rock. *That's* what He reiterated in my life through all of this. The moment we start thinking that *anything* else—even our congregation or our spiritual leaders—is a solid spiritual foundation we are in for an inevitable topple. While it is sometimes so easy to make tangible things and people our rocks, no institution or human being can successfully be our Lord without us ending up in the sand. "God is faithful" and, thanks to His grace and love, the faith of many from my former church only grew stronger in God and his Son, Jesus Christ. God alone is our foundation. We cannot worship a building of stone and mortar, nor a pastor, elder, or deacon. They may be humble, faithful, and kind servants of God, but they are still *not* God. Only God does not change. He is the Alpha and Omega, the Creator of all things, the Savior, the Redeemer, the Great Physician and Shepherd. He remains constant, never surprised or transformed by human tides.

Now, despite the pain of watching that church family fracture, most former members are living in faith and striving to follow Christ's call on their lives in many different corners of our city, other states, and even other countries. They have learned to turn only to Christ for spiritual sanctuary. "On Christ the solid rock I stand, *all* other ground is sinking sand. . . "

RELIGION AS AN IDOL

Let's revisit the Apostle Paul for a moment for a big picture example—an example of God working all things toward good for those who love Him and are called according to His purpose. Paul was a zealous Jew and Pharisee before Jesus struck him off of his donkey and *literally* blinded him to get his attention. Paul had made idols of the Jewish traditions created by teachers of the law—he was so encased by ritual that he had completely lost sight of God's promises of a messiah. To Paul, who practiced Hebrew law meticulously, the love, compassion, and grace of a new sect of Jews who followed the teachings of this Jesus (or Yeshua) from Nazareth were heretical and maniacal. After Paul's dramatic conversion to the Way, he followed Christ wholeheartedly and unabashedly for the rest of his life. But his life was anything but "blessed," judging by worldly expectations. In fact, in following Christ, Paul faced the same ridicule and physical suffering that other followers had once experienced at his hands; but he also experienced abundant joy, peace, and miracles as a result of his obedience. Paul faithfully preached the Word of the crucified and resurrected Christ, until he was beheaded by the Roman Emperor Nero because of his beliefs.

I dare say he never once imagined the impact and blessing his life would have on countless people for thousands of years to come. In light of Paul's ultimate destiny—and the blessing his life was, and still is, to so many—his trials as a Christian served an immense Godly purpose. They happened for a reason although, at the time, "purposeful" and "reasonable" were probably the last words he would have used to describe them. Read the list of his sufferings in 2 Corinthians 11:16-33 sometime. Many people, facing such trials, would have given up on their faith and thought that, perhaps, they had misheard the Lord in His calling. But they did not discourage Paul. He had been transformed—from a life of idolizing rituals and routines and man-written laws, to worshipping Christ. Diminutive and unattractive according to historians, Paul effected world change and was blessed beyond measure because he trusted Christ enough to "give up" the belief that religious routines and rituals would save him. The complete turnaround that God ordained in Paul's life—from Pharisee and tormentor of Christ-followers to zealous Christ-follower himself—and the teachings He inspired Paul to write in his letters became the backbone of the modern Christian church. What began as a life idolizing Jewish law and ceremony to the detriment of realizing truth, ended as a life well-lived for Jesus Christ and His coming kingdom. *

We are no different than Paul. It is *so* easy to fall into a lull of following the patterns, rituals, and habits developed by our "American church culture" and fail to make any real change in our society. We get caught up in superficial matters instead of focusing on loving people and sharing the good news. We become more concerned with the appearance of our communion elements than with remembering what they represent. We are distracted by which instrument is being played in our services instead of engaging in worship. We are distracted by our outward appearance in church rather than focused on examining our hearts. We generally think of idols as tangible

---

*Moore, Beth. *Paul: 90 Days on His Journey of Faith.* (Nashville, TN: B&H Publishing Group, 2010).

things—a wooden carving of Ganesha, a home we can't afford, a closet full of clothes representing credit card bills we haven't paid. While our culture is prone to excess, and "stuff" can overtake our lives and passions, consider for a moment that the idols that rule your heart may instead be intangible mindsets, rituals, and traditions that take the place of loving God and loving people.

Our human frame, crafted from dust, is limited in its flesh-pursuits. We are bound by the laws of nature and physics. If we rely wholly on ourselves—what we can understand, control, and achieve independent of a divine Creator—we are not only putting ourselves in the idol position, we are sorely limiting the potential our life has to make an eternal impact. However, that same crafted human form has been brought to life through the very breath of a loving Yahweh; a God-head with no limitations, no errors, no flaws. His expectations for us have been clearly laid out in His word. His love for us has been clearly displayed. Despite the parts of Him that we cannot understand or fathom, He has given us much hope, much knowledge, much love. Although God has bestowed upon us emotions, thoughts, and circumstances, none of these are meters of our faith or indicative of the depth of our spirituality. Our ultimate faith in God to guide us can exist in the midst of circumstances that provoke mourning, deep grief, and anger. Faith is the belief that God is who He says He is and that He can do what He says He can do. It is the trust that He is in control even when we don't understand the "whys." Faith is setting aside our own expectations and realizing that God's vision, ultimate purpose, and love are so much more abounding than our own that we can only get tiny glimpses of it this side of heaven. In the midst of this faith, God gives us the strength to keep getting out of bed when we don't feel like it; to trust Him, one day at a time; to experience joy along with pain; and to have gratitude, even in the midst of sorrow.

Chapter 4

Fulfillment and Growth

GOD'S GARDEN

In the late spring and early summer, when most people were landscaping, my husband and I were de-landscaping our side yard. Our lot, wooded along the edges of the property, had become extremely overgrown in the past few years from lack of upkeep. God began to draw parallels in my mind; I tore out weeds that had become trees and sawed down small trunks to level them to the ground. As the sweat ran down my back and my muscles burned, I began to compare this stubborn growth to the weeds of the mind.

When we let worldly ideas and expectations filter into our minds, they take root. We ignore them when they're small and growing because they seem harmless enough. It's easy to let them rest there, in the quiet, and turn to them to soothe us through disappointments or burdensome periods. We may even revel in the separation they provide from difficult things (like kudzu, they cover and insulate). Ultimately, though, the result is similar to what has happened to the eastern edge of my backyard: our minds become overgrown with those worldly desires, and they begin to choke off the growth of good things—the healthy fruit of Godly expectations our Father has planted. Like kudzu, they take over and block the light. As my observant daughter helped me bag up brush, small trunks, and twigs, she exclaimed, "Yard work is hard work!" What she doesn't realize yet is that pruning the mind can be even more difficult. When we let those attitudes and thoughts that conflict with God take root and grow, we miss God's path in the midst of the weeds. Even after we hear God's voice calling us back to His direction and begin to follow, it takes a lot more work to clear the weeds. And, as any gardener knows, they keep fighting back.

Like your garden-variety clover, many weeds of the mind look very pretty. Even the "good" ones, however, have no place in the well-manicured and flowered plot of "best" that God has planned for us. They don't fit into His blueprints for the landscape of our lives. You may have seen a home-improvement show featuring a team of landscaping experts who turn average backyards into a paradise in a matter of days. God can transform our hearts and renew our minds just like this team if we let Him. He can take the most barren or overgrown mind-yard and turn it into a beautiful garden with his supernatural cultivation. But, just like those unsuspecting couples wandering through home improvement stores must agree to trust the team to transform their plots of ground, we must first agree to turn our minds over to God.

When I was teaching full-time in public high school (my career plot, if you will), there was a still small voice in the back of my mind. It told me that *now* was the season to spend more time with my own children, to write ideas that had been forming in my heart and mind. As the days, weeks and months passed, it was apparent that I was supposed to leave full time teaching. I knew God wasn't asking me to leave teaching for good, only for a season, but it still required giving up a job that I loved despite its many difficulties, stigmas, and complaints. It required, for a time, giving up a salary that was a sure thing year-round. And it required the discipline and courage to devote myself to writing what God had put on my heart. My teaching job wasn't a "bad" weed. Teaching was "comfortable," it enabled me to be complacent because it was a "good thing." To the world, it was even laudable. But it wasn't the best for me in that particular season—it didn't fit into God's "now" plan. I am finding that although I obeyed God, it is not easier to cultivate my current plot. I have had to trust God to do some intensive mental weed pulling. Since I am following God's design, I trust it will eventually bloom beautifully—no matter how the outcome looks to others.

These days, I volunteer at my children's school, substitute teach, and write. Sometimes God wakes me in the middle of the night because there is something He wants me to record. I would have lamented this if I were still trying to teach full-time; I would have stressed out thinking of the coming school day and questioning whether I'd have the energy to patiently teach 90-minute blocks of ninth graders. Now I can cherish this alone time with God, when the rest of my family (dog included!) are still slumbering. God and I have such sweet times together. I also cherish the time I spend with my children now more than ever. I have more patience, more time to just sit, talk, play, and read. I am discovering so many wonderful things about these children God has entrusted to me.

I would have missed out on all of these joys if I had let the weeds of worry, complacency, or financial gain alone steer me from following God's calling. This season of my life is not without its struggles—I would be less than truthful if I didn't admit that there are days when I wonder, "*Why* did I resign again?" But then I remember. God has cleared the weeds in my brain so he could plant what He desired this season. I can breathe easily, trust Him, and know his current landscaping will yield something beautiful in time.

THE WEED OF PRIDE

There is a particular weed in my mental garden I have had to keep a sharp eye on—*pride*. Even after vigorously working to fight worry and complacency, I find this pesky pride growth coming back. Unlike the mental image I think we often have of an angry Creator, stripping our pride away from us using embarrassing or vengeful methods, our true Father God is long-suffering, compassionate, and tears down my pride gently—for He is gentle with His children. He is showing me many areas of my life that need work, areas that I had not noticed before. He is changing my habit of expectation and constantly showing me that *He* is God and I am *not*. Anyone who does not believe that God is a God of humor and concrete lessons, read on!

I spent a morning testing reading levels and counting ability in a kindergarten class. My six-foot frame was uncomfortably perched on a child-sized chair in a busy, stuffy hallway. I gave ecstatic nods and smiles as the five-year-olds proudly displayed their knowledge to me, often adding their own personal anecdotes to the academic comments. The funniest boy (who was also the highest counter) punctuated his numerical performance with hilarious sidebars about the people in the hallway, his family, and life in general. He was so obviously bored with mere counting that he just had to throw other things into the mix. Sitting on those little chairs, I learned lessons about humility and God was also showing me, first-hand, the child-like wonder, curiosity, trust, and excitement that He wants us to have for Him. Nobody can teach us like a child—they are living testaments in putting aside our pride, living life with whole-hearted joy, and trusting in things bigger than ourselves.

From an adult perspective, teaching young children can seem tedious: it requires nose-wiping, shoe-tying, and belaboring over rudimentary skills. A kindergarten teacher cannot be filled with self-swelling pride, because her calling often requires her to deal directly with the "dirty," "messy," or "mundane." I wonder if God ever feels like a kindergarten teacher when He deals with us. As believers, God calls us to put aside our pride and love others the same way kindergarten teachers love their students. It is sometimes a dirty job, and far from glamorous. We must sometimes do things "below our dignity." But the results of putting aside our pride to follow God and love people are priceless. Believers are occasionally under the false impression that enduring the "mundane" of our daily lives is somehow beneath us. We look at the messier parts of loving people in need and begin to think we are above it all. We are hopelessly misled. But we can find joy if we let go of the pride in our own "positions" and embrace, wholeheartedly and with the grace of Christ, all of the business of faith — even the trickier parts, like getting our hands dirty in the name of showing grace and kindness to those God created.

HUMBLE YOURSELVES

Pride moves stealthily. It is tricky and elusive. It can conquer us when it lessens or removes our capacity to love, forgive, show compassion, and exude joy. Sometimes, pride keeps us from making a change that we are supposed to make; other times, it moves us when we should stay. Pride has been known to keep people from blessings because a task seemed "beneath them;" and has led other people—too confident in their own abilities—to fall. Pride keeps people from mending relationships, or even developing them in the first place.

Conquering pride means being able to say: "I made a mistake," "You were right and I was wrong," or "I will do that menial task." Conquering pride also means being able to say, "I love you anyway," "I forgive you," and "Let's do this together." Some of those phrases make us feel uneasy—we think that uttering them would be a sign of weakness, when they really require enormous strength. Admitting that we messed up, that we're afraid, or that we simply don't know what to do means putting aside our pride and being real. It's too bad that we are often more concerned with perception than reality. We want people to perceive us a certain way and, if pride keeps the perception alive, we will let it rule us. This is dangerous because pride is a slithering snake; it is shifting sand upon which to build our lives. When we let pride rule our decisions, we often make the wrong ones. In attempting to be perceived as strong in our power, intellect, or ability, we are soon swept off our feet into the sand.

Not everybody struggles with pride. Many people are exactly where they should be, doing what God has called them to do, and making a difference—I've met people who aren't afraid of the messiness of unconditional love. I have always admired these people, because they are usually filled to the brim with joy and able to pour it over the people around them. They also are forgiving, compassionate, and *humble* people. When we conquer pride and seek humility, we receive blessings and comfort from the Lord. Psalm 25:9 says that God "guides the humble in what is right and teaches them His way." God often uses other people to guide us. First Peter 5:5-6 beseeches the young to "submit yourselves to your elders. All of you, clothe yourselves with humility toward one another, because 'God opposes the proud, but shows favor to the humble.'" God encourages mentorships, friendships, and discipleship. We are not meant to walk alone, and we don't have to as long as false pride has been banished from our hearts.

A WINDOW TO THE HEART

Driving my children to school on certain October mornings, my van strains to the crest of a hill and I am suddenly blinded by the sunlight that reflects across my entire windshield, like a spot light at a concert. Up to this point in my drive, my windshield has seemed perfectly clean and my vision through it is unimpaired. However, this sudden glare illuminates the dirty fingerprints, bits of dead insect, and other unknown substances on the glass that are clouding up my vision. One day, I was struck by a comparison. My heart often seems "clean" (or "in the right place") but, when viewed in the all-encompassing light of the Father, it shows smudges that weren't there before.

There are thousands of quotes from many cultures about the human heart. Many of the best-known ones come from the Bible: "A cheerful heart is good medicine. . . " (Proverbs 17:22); "As water reflects a face, so one's life reflects the heart" (Proverbs 27:19); "... the mouth speaks what the heart is full of" (Matthew 12:34); "People look at the outward appearance, but the Lord looks at the heart." (1 Samuel 16:7); "The heart is deceitful above all things and beyond cure; who can understand it?" (Jeremiah 17:9). God looks at our true motivations and devotion when he looks at our hearts; are we living to please God, or men? He knows our thoughts and our pursuits. If we rely on our emotions to guide us in place of God, then we will be deceived. Our emotions change like the tides and, like the tides, they can be deceptive. They can appear to be rolling one way while an undercurrent is running the other. Our "windshield" may look perfectly clean from one angle, but from another, it is a mess.

When God said that He "looks at the heart," He sees our true loyalty and devotion. Our Creator and Father knows we aren't perfect, but He also knows if we are pursuing Him. God knew David was a man after His own heart. He knew that David's motivation was to follow God and trust Him completely (how he handled Goliath is proof of that). If you delve into David's life story, you know that he was far from perfect—he made emotionally-driven decisions that caused grave consequences. God knew from the beginning that

David would commit adultery, and command a murder, and God was direct with David about his specific punishment for those actions. What I love about the gracious God of the Hebrews is what followed the consequences of David's sins: grace. God did not abandon David, nor did He halt His plan for the lives of David or his sons.

Like the light of the sun on my windshield, the light of the Son on my heart causes me to do two things: focus all of my attention on the light and see the true condition of my heart. It makes me all the more grateful for God's love and grace. When He shines His light on me, my expectations for my life move more into line with His own. He shows me what I need to let go, and to what I need to hold fast. If it weren't for God's boundless love and the grace He bestows freely, none of us would measure up. We have all harbored specks over our hearts—unfair judgments, hatred, assumptions, bitterness, and unforgiveness. God shines His light on us to both expose the darkness and reflect His own perfection. If you think about it, to those inside a car the light of the autumn sun is temporarily blinding; it keeps the driver and passengers from seeing anything *but* the dirty windshield. All anyone outside the vehicle can see, however, is the reflection of the sun. As believers, God expects us to reflect Him, and let his light show us where we need to change from the inside out.

One day, as we drove home from worship, God pointed out to me trees along our route. Some had been completely devoid of leaves for weeks, but some still bravely blazed with fiery red and orange foliage. Others seemed to think it was the throes of summer—in the midst of fall color and winter decay, they were covered with green leaves. I began to think about how people are like trees. In this walk called life, we often compare ourselves to others. We look around and see the ways our life differs from theirs and we begin asking questions. "Why them, not me?" we wonder. "Why is my career not going like theirs? Why do I seem less fulfilled than they do? Why is my life harder? Why do they seem to have it all together when I don't? How come their spiritual life is so secure and grounded and mine is not?" Sometimes the answer to these questions lies in our hearts, habits, and discipline; other times the fluctuations are attributable to "seasons" in our lives.

I remember when my son was about six months old and I was struggling with some small thing at the time—either my son's lack of a sleeping schedule or the fact that he eschewed the bottle and absolutely insisted on being nursed for every feeding. My friend Emily gave me comfort: "Don't worry. Everything's a phase." It struck me as profound at the time, but God still hadn't finished with that message. A few years later, a mentor of mine observed that life was full of different seasons, but God *never* leaves us.

As I observed the trees during the ride home from church, that lesson came back to me anew. In a particularly tenuous season of life, there are monumental decisions to be made and I often feel frozen, unable to make the correct choices. I have sat on the throne as the queen of second-guessing. I've questioned facets of my life. I've analyzed myself until tears flow without reason. But those trees reassured me. Seeing their varicolored foliage (or complete lack thereof!) I was reminded that I am unique. I was reminded that, like David, God knows the motivations of my heart and covers me with grace. And I realized this season will pass, like so many others have before. Whether I am content or in longing, God is with me; *nothing* can tear me from his hands. Someday I will look back on this season of my life and wonder why I was so panicked—like I now look back at the time when my children were babies and wonder why I was so concerned then about things that seem so minor in retrospect.

God works throughout our seasons, to grow us into His image. We will have winters, when we don't move forward much. But we will also have springs. God will create some new work in us, or lead us to a new revelation about who He is, and we will grow like crazy. We will bear much fruit in our spiritual summers, but there will still be autumnal seasons—where the days are darker and colder, and we shed ungodly weeds like the fall leaves. This shedding may leave us feeling bare and exposed; but even when we shiver and feel cold towards God, He is always there. The cycle will come around again. God will birth something new in us and, with it, new fire and new zest for life. We have to remember that, like the trees, we are all different. Our life lessons look different because we are unique, and we cycle through lessons from God at different paces. Some believers experience incredibly long springs and summers. Others feel like their falls and winters last way too long.

There's something else important that I noticed about those trees: whether they were bare, blazing, or still green, they were all standing proudly, their limbs lifted up to the sun. So I learned another lesson today: whether I am emotionally bare, spiritually blazing, or experiencing a shedding of things that hinder, all God calls me to do is lift my arms to Him in worship. All He asks is for me to look up to the Son and stand tall in His love. I can be secure that God knows me intimately, loves me dearly, and is still leading me along the path He's marked out for me.

ABOUT THE AUTHOR

Gretchen Huff is a high school teacher by trade and has taught both part time and full time for the past 17 years in West Africa, four Middle Tennessee high schools, and a home school tutorial/cooperative. She is married to Jason Huff. They have two children, Ben and Chelsea. This is her first book.

Connect with Gretchen through her blog "Write Now" at gretchenhuff.wordpress.com and on Facebook at facebook.com/writenow.gretchen.

ACKNOWLEDGEMENTS AND CREDITS

Thanks first to Beck Sharp, who took a mess of ideas and organized them into something readable. Many thanks to Kyra Barger for knowing exactly what I was looking for in the cover photo and capturing it brilliantly within a few hours. Also, thanks to Gwen Adams. Without her technical knowledge of e-book publishing and sharp eye for last-minute editing, Idol Life would not be in your hands. Lastly, thanks to Erica Manly for designing the spine and backcover of the printed book.

Cover Photograph: Kyra Barger, Faso Photography (www.fasophotography.com)

Design and PressBooks Integration: Gwen Adams, Kudzu Garden Media (facebook.com/kudzugarden)

ADDITIONAL ACKNOWLEDGEMENT

An additional thanks to Erica Manly. I was completely befuddled by the design technology necessary to create a back cover and spine for the print version of this book, but Erica completed it in a few hours it looks GREAT!